# Baptism

## Christ's Act
## in the Church

# Baptism

## Christ's Act
## in the Church

Laurence Hull Stookey

ABINGDON
Nashville

## BAPTISM: CHRIST'S ACT IN THE CHURCH

*Copyright © 1982 by Abingdon*

**Library of Congress Cataloging in Publication Data**

STOOKEY, LAURENCE HULL, 1937-
  Baptism, Christ's act in the church.
  Includes bibliographical references and index.
  1. Baptism I. Title.
  BV811.2.S86      234'.161      81-17590      AACR2

**ISBN 0-687-02364-5**

MANUFACTURED BY THE PARTHENON PRESS AT
NASHVILLE, TENNESSEE, UNITED STATES OF AMERICA

For
LAURA ANN
and
SARAH ELIZABETH


that they may know the meaning of their baptism
and be thankful

# CONTENTS

# ACKNOWLEDGMENTS

Every book is, in some sense, a corporate effort. In many books, those who contributed have their names listed in the acknowledgments. But in this instance, a large number of people will have to be content with anonymity; for the list would be too extensive to include, even if it were possible to compile.

First, there are the many students both in the seminary and in continuing education programs who have sharpened my theology, and forced me to think in terms of concrete parish situations. They have, I hope, been successful in this task.

Then there are those who, in groups charged with the responsibility for creating new liturgical forms, responded to the drafts of these rites that I had been asked to prepare. Members of the task force that produced the alternate text on baptism, confirmation, and renewal for The United Methodist Church were incredibly adept at pinning me to the wall, and forcing me to justify or surrender every syllable that went into that document. That was (if I may be forgiven the phrase) my baptism by fire; traumatic at the time, it has been immensely valuable since. Originally, that group envisioned a longer publication than for economic reasons we finally had the courage to produce; much of what is in this book is footage from the cutting-room floor of that venture.

For the worship commission of The Consultation on Church Union, I was the principal writer of *An Order of Thanksgiving for the Birth or Adoption of a Child.* Members of that commission and its sub-committee on pre- and post-baptismal rites were also perceptive in their criticism, and encouraging in their support of the work.

I have also been greatly helped by participation in three projects involving ecumenical theological dialogue. I am indebted to those I worked with over a period of three years in the national Lutheran-United Methodist Bilateral Consultation on baptism. Much was also gained at the 1979 international consultation of Baptists and non-Baptists sponsored by the Faith and Order Section of the World Council of Churches. I was further stimulated by other members of the team that drafted for The United Methodist Church a formal response to the World Council document, *One Baptism, One Eucharist, and a Mutually Recognized Ministry,* and by representatives of many denominations in the United States, who later gathered to suggest revisions of the same document, preparatory to the World Council's Sixth Assembly in 1983. To the members of all of these groups I express deep gratitude, though they cannot be mentioned specifically.

Some who have contributed to this joint venture can be named, however. Encouragement to write this book came particularly from the Rev. Hoyt L. Hickman, Assistant General Secretary of the Board of Discipleship of The United Methodist Chuch, and from Professor James F. White of Perkins School of Theology; both through their general work with the denomination's Section on Worship and through their specific comments on the manuscript, they have assisted me greatly. The initial manuscript was also read and commented upon by colleagues in related theological disciplines: Dr. David L. Tiede, Professor of New Testament at Luther-Northwestern Theological Seminaries; and Dr. James C. Logan, Professor of Systematic Theology at Wesley Theological Seminary. Their corrective insights have meant much. Special thanks is due to Dr. Kendall K. McCabe, Assistant Professor of Homiletics and Worship at United Theological Seminary, Dayton; before assuming that post, he did double duty toward the completion of this book. By teaching my classes while I was on sabbatical leave, he enabled me to write with the assurance that my usual duties were being covered admirably; he also read the manuscript, and made detailed comments on it. In addition to being contributors to this book, these colleagues have the dubious distinction of experiencing first-hand Stookey's Law of Academic Leave: "Professors who are on sabbatical scheme to devise ways to create additional work for professors who are not on leave."


LAURENCE HULL STOOKEY


WESLEY THEOLOGICAL SEMINARY
WASHINGTON, D.C.

# PROLOGUE

Early in this century, a baby born in England, Lucille by name, was taken by her maternal grandmother to the local Wesleyan chapel to be baptized. Lucy's father, a sturdy Anglican, was skeptical about the whole proceeding since the Church of England does not regard Methodist clergy as being in the apostolic succession. So he took Lucy to the Anglican parish church where she was baptized again. Now Lucy's mother was a convert to the Salvation Army and didn't think much of either the Wesleyans or the Anglicans. So she took Lucy to the local citadel for presentation under the banner of blood and fire—the Salvationist counterpart to baptism.

In time the family emigrated to the midwestern United States. The community they moved into had neither an Episcopal Church nor an Army Citadel; so the family attended the Methodist Church. As a teenager, Lucy joined a class of those preparing to take the vows of church membership. Now it happened that the pastor was one of those mavericks who looks upon the practices of his own denomination with disapproval, and regards the baptism of infants as a misguided tradition. He therefore decreed that all in the class had to be "truly baptized" at the font on the day of their vows. Lucy's mother discovered what was afoot and said, "Absolutely not. Three times is enough for anyone." But Lucy was a good psychologist and knew that once her mother was seated in church, she would not make a scene. When the rest of the group went to the font, so did Lucy!

Now it came to pass that some years later Lucy fell in love with, and married, a Southern Baptist—but not without extracting from him a pledge that she need not be baptized yet again. He agreed that she was quite sufficiently initiated into the church, and all was well—until they moved to a community where they attended a Baptist Church that was in need of a pianist. Lucy loved to play, and seemed to be a providential gift to the congregation. But, ruled the deacons solemnly and steadfastly, unimmersed hands may not play the Lord's songs for us. And so, for the fifth time, Lucy was initiated into Christ's church.[1]

Whether or not she deserves a place in the *Guinness Book of Records,* I have not determined. But this much is certain: behind Lucy's experience lie assumptions that have been made by Christians from time to time—that baptism with water is not a necessary rite, nor even a helpful one, but is better replaced by a more spiritual ceremony that does not rely on sacramental signs (the assumption of Lucy's mother); that baptism is constituted by a particular denomination, or at least depends upon the apostolic succession of ministers within certain denominations (the assumption of Lucy's father); that baptism can be administered properly only after a person reaches a certain age (the assumption of Lucy's pastor in the Midwest); that baptism is dependent upon the manner in which the water is administered (the assumption of the Baptist deacons). All of these assumptions will be called into question in the course of this book. But we cannot begin there.

These assumptions pertain to the human side of the rite of baptism. Unless we start from the other side, we will simply compound the confusion. For above all else, baptism is a gift from God to the church. If it is not, why make such a fuss about it? We may as well abolish the practice, and thus put an end to the confusion and competing notions that surround it. Baptism is God's gift to the church, Christ's act within the church. This is a fundamental assumption. Now we must try to make sense of such a bold assertion.

# 1

# BAPTISM: CHRIST'S ACT IN THE CHURCH

## SPIRITUAL AMNESIA AND GOD'S STORY

Each of us suffers from spiritual amnesia. We forget what God has done for us and promised to us. We also conveniently forget what God wants of us as disciples. In short, we are oblivious to the identity we have been given by our Creator. God, aware of our malady and of our inability to effect a cure (or even to recognize the impairment), acts to reveal our true identity to us.

One means by which God counteracts this amnesia is baptism. Yet so pervasive is our disability that often we forget God's activity in this sacrament and see baptism merely as a human action: a symbol of our devotion to God, an enacted affirmation of faith. Baptism is that, but it is much more. To understand the sacrament in its fullness, we need to begin with the divine side, with God's action toward us. Through baptism, God tells us the story of divine love—a story which, for the sake of natural memory, may be summarized under five headings: creation, covenant, Christ, church, and coming kingdom. We shall examine each in turn.

Through the water of baptism, God brings to our remembrance the stories of the early chapters of Genesis: creation itself, at which the Spirit brooded over the chaotic waters, dividing and restraining them so that land could appear; the rivers of the Garden of Eden; and the deluge of Noah's day, by means of which God again contended with chaos and brought forth a re-created world. The stories of creation presented to us through the water of baptism bring to our attention central themes of the gospel that enable us to know who we are—and whose we are.

13

In the account of creation, we discover that God is active in our world, and that we are responsible creatures made in the image of God. In the story of the Fall, God holds before us a mirror so that we may see ourselves as rebellious creatures who are nevertheless loved and protected by the Creator. Here we glimpse the paradox of our existence: that we can be truly free only by renouncing a life that centers upon self-interest and by willingly taking up the cross of obedience, which outwardly appears to promise nothing more than servitude and death. In calling to our remembrance the story of the flood, God further reveals the mystery of divine judgment and grace; the same water that destroys sin buoys up the ark and sets it down in safety so righteousness may flourish. Thus, we discover that we are at once judged and saved by the One who has made us. Through baptism, God reveals to us our identity as redeemed creatures.

God also shows us our identity by presenting us with the experience of covenant. A covenant initiates a relationship between one who makes a promise (often someone of superiority or authority) and those to whom the promise is given.

Through the water of baptism, God brings to our attention the covenant made with Noah after the flood: "Behold, I establish my covenant with you and your descendants after you, and with every living creature that is with you . . . that never again shall all flesh be cut off by the waters of a flood" (Gen. 9:8-11).

God also reminds us of the covenant with Israel, which was accompanied by many events involving water: the crossing of the sea, the cloud that guided the people, the water brought forth from the rock in the wilderness, the bitter waters of Marah and the sweet springs of Elim, and the crossing of the Jordan into the land of promise. If our spiritual amnesia causes us to think that connections between our baptism and the ancient deluge and Exodus are fanciful, we need to recall their New Testament basis. Peter saw an unambiguous link between baptism and the flood (I Peter 3:18-22); and to such an extent did the earliest Christians identify baptism with passing through the waters of bondage and death that Paul could write of the Hebrews that "they were all baptized into Moses in this cloud and in this sea; . . . all drank from the spiritual rock that followed them as they went, and that rock was Christ" (I Cor. 10:1-4, Jerusalem Bible). The apostle did not mean that the Hebrews actually participated in a baptismal rite, for they did not; but Paul intended us to see that both they and we find release from captivity through the grace of the God of covenants.[1]

Covenant-making was often accompanied by a sign given to aid the remembrance of the divine promise. Thus, the rainbow was the sign of the covenant with Noah, and the Passover lamb was the sign of the covenant with Israel. Baptism is itself a covenant God initiates with us; the water is the sign given to us to help us remember the promise of the Lord, and to remind us of our identity as a responsible people.

All that was prepared for, and anticipated, in creation and in the Old Testament covenants came to fulfillment in Jesus Christ. Indeed, it is Christ himself who presents us with the water of baptism, thus gathering up the whole of the Old Testament story and revealing its purpose in his own person. That Christ gathers all of this into himself is reflected in Ephesians 1:9-10: "For [God] has made known to us in all wisdom and insight the mystery of his will, according to his purpose which he has set forth in Christ, as a plan for the fulness of time, to unite all things in him, things in heaven and things on earth." What the RSV translates as "unite" is the Greek term *anakephalaiosasthai,* meaning to recapitulate; it is the equivalent of the Latin term *recapitulare.* In baptism, this recapitulation is made visible as Christ, active in the water, presents the full story of his work.

The water of Christian initiation brings with it a multitude of associations surrounding the Incarnation. The life and ministry of Jesus were bracketed by water. At the beginning, he was nurtured in the water of Mary's womb and baptized in the Jordan. At the end, he cried out in thirst from the cross, and the centurion's spear emptied him of the very substances of life—blood and water. Jesus' ministry began around the Sea of Galilee where he called disciples as they mended their nets, where he walked upon the water and stilled the storm. Jesus used aquatic imagery frequently in his preaching, speaking of the God who sends rain on the just and the unjust, of the signs of weather in the sky, and of the cup of cold water given in his name. Particularly in John's Gospel, the work of Jesus is associated with water. There his first miracle is that of turning water into wine; at Jacob's well he meets the Samaritan woman, and tells her that he himself is the water of life. In Jerusalem, he heals the paralyzed man at the side of the pool; he restores sight to the man born blind by making clay with saliva, and then sends the man to bathe in the pool of Siloam. Jesus washes the feet of his followers before his passion; and after his resurrection, he grants a marvelous catch of fish to the disciples.

Nothing in creation has the power to remind us so fully of the work of our Lord as the common substance of water. This he gives us at baptism as a token of his saving grace, so that from the time of our initiation onward we may be reminded of all he has done for us, so that we may see ourselves as a people united to him and to one another in him.

Christ constitutes the church by the power of the Holy Spirit. The church is the community of his covenant, his family, the sons and daughters of God, adopted by grace. Baptism is the sign of the covenant, the sign of the birth that is not of flesh and blood but that comes as a gift from above. The sign is shared by virtually all Christians, and thus is a bond of union between each Christian and all others who are in Christ.

Baptism belongs to the church; no other organization or society practices it. Yet baptism is not the church's act, but Christ's act in the church. And although baptism is Christ's initiation of us into his family, its meaning is by no means confined to the time of its administration. Baptism pushes us into the future, even as it helps us to understand the tradition of the church and to live as contemporary disciples. Much more will be said in later chapters about the nature of the church as Christ's baptized people; here it is sufficient to emphasize that baptism is a sign of identity Christ gives the church, lest we forget that we are God's people, and become content to be just another human organization. The sacrament is a gift given by the power of the Holy Spirit to the community of the Spirit.

In Jesus Christ, the kingdom of God has already come into our midst. The church (in a regrettably imperfect way) is an extension of the kingdom-presence in the world. Jesus instructed us to wait expectantly for the coming of the kingdom in its fullness; in the Lord's Prayer we pray continually for this coming of the kingdom. Even so, the anxieties of life dim our vision of the future, and we are prone to forget the hope that characterizes the gospel. Therefore, in baptism, Christ gives the church a sign of his ultimate reign over all things. Baptism points to the future even more than to the past. For what God has done in creation, in covenant-making, in the coming of Christ, and in the establishment of the church by the power of the Holy Spirit—all of this presses on toward the fulfillment of the divine purpose in history.

Various biblical writers envisioned the coming of the kingdom in ways that enter the spiritual memory through baptism. Perhaps none of these visions is more striking than that of John on Patmos; for The Revelation often speaks of the sea, the rainbow, the water of life, and other aquatic imagery in relation to Christ's rule over all things. Baptism is a gift from Christ that can overcome our tendency to forget the hope we have in him and in his final triumph over sin and death.

## BAPTISM AND THE MEANING OF GOD'S STORY

Creation, covenant, Christ, church, and coming kingdom are not separate entities. All are pervaded by common meanings that help us know who we are before God. We now look at some of these common clues to our identity as they point to divine purpose.

Like every good story, the biblical story has a beginning and an end as well as a middle. In the water of baptism, God sets before us both the start and the conclusion of the divine story, thus revealing the purpose of this movement from creation to consummation.

In the beginning, there exists nothing but the water of chaos; this God contains within the seas (Gen. 1:9-10). In the end, even the sea is destroyed (Rev. 21:1). In the beginning, God creates light and later makes of it the sun and the moon for the firmament (Gen. 1:3, 14-15). In the end, there is no need for sun or moon; for the very glory of God enlightens all

(Rev. 21:23). At the first, there is a garden of paradise with trees and a river, and at the last, there is again a great tree of life and a river pure as crystal; but instead of a garden for two persons, there is finally a city that can accommodate the whole company of the redeemed.[2] The end of the story represents progress and expansion, not merely a recovery or repetition of the beginning.

Through baptism, God tells us that history is headed somewhere. We are now between the river of Eden and the river of the heavenly city; but we are not wandering aimlessly. We are moving from one to the other. God has a purpose, and pursues it relentlessly. In the end, that purpose will be accomplished. In this assurance we have hope and life.

God's purpose is characterized by faithfulness in the face of human fickleness. God did not abandon Adam and Eve, but protected them after the Fall and extended the same protection to Cain. Although the flood destroyed the wicked in Noah's time, it also preserved the righteous—as did the water of the sea at the Exodus. Noah so abused the renewed creation by over-indulgence that his sons found him in a drunken stupor. His sons were no saints, either; their sin led to the debacle of the Tower of Babel. Yet the promises of God stood. After being released from the grasp of Pharaoh, Israel again and again proved unfaithful to God; yet Yahweh was faithful to Israel. The water from the rock in the wilderness was not a response to an intense faith but a response to a rebellious murmuring by the people. The resurrection of Jesus Christ is God's response to the murder of the One sent to us from above. Christians in every age have had ample evidence that within the church sin co-exists with the gift of the Spirit. God is like a lover who waits out the infidelity of the beloved, like parents who yearn for the return of an errant child. The consistent witness of Scripture is that the kingdom will come in its fullness, not because we merit it, but because God is faithful. This the water of baptism proclaims, for it sets before us a witness to divine persistence.

The God who is faithful is no pushover, however. Grace implies judgment, not the lack of it. Baptism announces that we do not have an "anything goes" God. Adam and Eve were expelled from Eden, and Cain became a fugitive. The sea covered the wicked of Noah's day, and the chariots and horsemen of Pharaoh. Israel tarried in the wilderness forty years because of sin, and centuries later was taken captive because of disregard for the covenant. The church has ever confessed that Christ died because of sin, and the glories of the last chapters of The Revelation are preceded by accounts of the agonies of the end. The God who seeks the salvation of the sinner nevertheless requires the destruction of the sin.

Water has a unique capacity to convey this inseparability of grace and judgment. A sufficient quantity of water can assuage thirst or provide opportunity for recreation and commerce. But too little water, or too much, can cause death by dehydration, or by drowning, can destroy boating and shipping activities, whether by drought that leaves docks inaccessible, or by devastating storms that sweep them away in a single night. Within a few verses, the author of The Revelation speaks of "the springs of living water" and of the water which caused many to die "because it was bitter" (Rev. 7:17; 8:11). Through baptism, Christ reveals a God who is neither cruelly vindictive nor sentimentally indulgent. The God whose people we are is both the constant foe of unrighteousness and the trustworthy giver of holiness. The grace of God is characterized by a toughness that demands the transformation of all that is imperfect.

God's ultimate purpose, then, is to bring into our midst that newness to which Scripture consistently testifies. The physical creation was itself a new work of God. Through the flood, sinful creation was renewed. Covenants established new relationships. Frequently those who were the beneficiaries of God's covenants received new names: Abram and Sarai became Abraham and Sarah; Jacob became Israel, and his personal name was later bestowed upon the whole covenant people. In biblical terms, a new name implies a new identity, a personality made new by the power of God. It is of particular importance that God, in initiating the covenant with Moses and the people in Egypt, gave them a new understanding by revealing the divine name YHWH—a name surrounded by the mystery and the majesty that distinguish the living God from the idols (Ex. 3:13-15).

Jesus Christ is newness incarnate. He is the "new Adam"

19

whose coming is the dawning of a new age (I Cor. 15:45; Luke 1:78).[3] He is the "first-born of many" who through him are made sons and daughters of God (Rom. 8:29). In the sacrifice on the cross, the Lord recapitulates and fulfills the sacrifice of the paschal lamb; and thus, as the Lamb of God, he institutes the new covenant in his own blood (I Cor. 5:7-8; 11:25).

The church is the community of the new covenant. Those within it are a new creation (II Cor. 5:17; Gal. 6:15). The church anticipates the coming of a new heaven and a new earth governed by One who sits upon the throne and says, "Behold, I make all things new" (Rev. 21:1, 5).

What God communicates to us through baptism enables us to look at life in a new way, and so to make sense of it. Thoughtful people have always been troubled by the power and persistence of evil in the world and by the disparity between human ideals and achievements. The story God tells us in baptism reveals that, in a way we may not fully grasp, chaos serves a divine purpose for a time. Ultimately God will openly exercise divine dominion over all that is disorderly and disruptive; until then, the chaotic forces of the universe have their boundaries set, even as do the waters of the sea, and are used to God's purpose in the communication of grace. In terms of the biblical story recalled in baptism, God does not cause sin or evil; nor does God stand helpless before them. God engages in a destructive-creative process. In the end, sin and death will be totally destroyed. Of this we can be confident, because our Lord's death and resurrection presages and effects that total annihilation and inaugurates the kingdom.

In the saving work of Jesus Christ, the new creation has begun. In baptism, the waters of life are already given to us in an anticipatory way. The fullness of the new creation is not yet apparent; yet by faith in the promise of God, we already experience its reality. Despite the sinful nature of its members, the church constituted through baptism shares in the nature of the heavenly city which is coming. Because the heavenly kingdom is open to all, the church on earth seeks to be a truly catholic community. Human tendencies to prefer groups which are homogeneous culturally, economically, racially, and politically are challenged by the newness Christians find in baptism. God's grace impels the church to be on earth what the church is to be in heaven.

The baptized are not surprised to find sin in the church; neither are they reluctant to pursue goals that seem unattainable. We know that we walk in the land between the river of Eden and the river of heaven; we know in which direction God has headed us and by what grace we will reach the destination. Through the water of the sacrament, God has revealed to us the purpose and progress of creation.

## CHRIST'S SIGN AND ACT

We have noted the biblical covenant-making was often accompanied by the giving of signs. We now need to look more closely at the nature and implications of the sign God grants us in baptism. Signs have four characteristics that are of particular interest to us.

(a) Signs are God's message mediated through the created world. They are physical in nature, and thus speak to us of the faithfulness of the Creator, despite our frequent disregard for, or even destruction of, creation. Signs assure us that God does not stand off from the world but works through it.

In some religious systems, there is a tendency to look upon the physical world with suspicion or even hostility. In the Western tradition, thinking was been greatly influenced by ancient religions that considered matter to be opposed to spirit. The Greeks, for example, tended to think of the world as a kind of prison from which the soul must be freed in order to be united with God. In the *Timaeus,* Plato attributed creation, not to the great deity, but to a lesser god, the "demiurge," who simply did the best that could be done with the corrupt materials available. Lucretius, in *The Nature of the Universe (De rerum natura),* stated bluntly that the world was not created by divine power at all, as its imperfections make apparent.

Such views have tended to obscure for us the Hebraic understanding of the unity and goodness of creation. We find evidence of this in the pious inclination to underemphasize the humanity of Jesus for fear that somehow his human nature diminishes his divinity. Similarly, many sincere Christians suspect that while sacraments may be fine for the weak in faith who need physical assurance as a kind of crutch, those who are mature in faith should have outgrown dependence upon material things such as water, bread, and wine.

Such over-spiritualization is not biblical, however; nor is it even true to human experience in our daily lives. When those whom we love are ill or grief-stricken, we send them cards, flowers, and food; we visit them because we know that physical presence is important. On birthdays and anniversaries we plan parties with food, decorations, and music. Why? Because God has created us with an appreciation for the physical world, and has given us the material order of things as a gift. Christians know the world around us can be a means of revelation.

(b) The material world *can* be a means of revelation; yet it is not necessarily so. For there is a second important characteristic to signs. Signs have about them a hidden quality; or at least they are easily overlooked and taken for granted. Those things God gives us as signs can be interpreted in various ways. For example, to the community of faith, a rainbow may be seen as a visible reminder of God's love; but to those outside of that community (even to many within it), a rainbow is simply the refraction of light through droplets of water—a natural phenomenon any child can produce in miniature with a garden hose on a sunny day. To those outside of the Christian faith, washing with water may serve only hygienic and aesthetic needs; but to those who are in Christ, that washing we call baptism is nothing less than God's communication to us, a divine sign of grace which gives life.

(c) This leads to the third characteristic of God's signs. They are not intended to force faith upon the skeptical, but rather to elicit and reinforce faith within the covenant community. The Bible does on occasion talk about signs that seem intended to convince the scoffers; but such signs are not given in the context of covenant-making, and almost never do they succeed. Again and again, for example, Moses and Aaron go to Pharaoh with marvelous signs; but the king's own magicians can imitate most of these. In the end, such signs do not persuade Pharaoh to let the Hebrews go. Jesus spurned the demand for miracles that would compel faith and warned against relying upon them. We find examples in passages such as Mark 8:11-12 and parallels, Luke 17:20, John 4:48, and John 12:37. God's signs are not for those who doubt divine love and want to be convinced by spectacular means. Signs are for those who suffer spiritual amnesia and are willing to look for God at work in the world around them, that they may thus discover the identity God has for them.

(d) The final characteristic of God's signs is that they represent life given freely and abundantly. The material sign of the covenant with Noah was the rainbow; we have noted the life-giving quality of water. The material sign of the covenant with Abraham and Sarah was circumcision, a rather explicit reference to the anatomical-physiological source of life. The material sign of the covenant with the Hebrews in Egypt was the blood of the lamb upon the doors of their houses and the Passover meal on the flesh of that lamb; the sacrificial offering of the life of an animal spared and nourished the life of the faithful.

It is important that the central signs of the covenant of Christ—water, bread, and wine—are abundant as well as life-giving. It is of no small consequence that the sacramental elements are not caviar and champagne nor that rare substance which scientists call "heavy water." The ordinariness of daily food and drink indicates that God's life is freely offered to all.

The signs God gives us are to be received in a particular order. Jesus Christ is God's great sign. All other signs flow from him. Even the signs of the Old Testament proceed from Christ—not from the Incarnate One, to be sure, but from the eternal Christ, the first-born of all creation who is "before all things" and in whom "all things hold together" (Col. 1:15-17). The incarnate coming of Christ exemplified fully the four characteristics of signs. He came into the natural order, born of woman—fully human, as our creeds insist. His revelation had and has a certain hiddenness to it. His own disciples did not recognize him for who he was until after his resurrection; and today many regard him simply as a good teacher and a martyr, not unlike Socrates. The Incarnate One did not compel faith, though always he invited it to spring forth. He freely gave his own life for the life of the whole world. He is the first and great sign of God to the world—not merely to the church, but to the world.

From the world, Christ has gathered a company of those who understand him to be God's sign. This company is the church, which is itself by derivation a sign to the world. The church does not exist for itself, but for the sake of others in whose midst it is to be a colony of heaven. Thus, the church shares the characteristics of a sign. Whatever else it may be, the church is a sociological phenomenon with traits common to all such institutions. Therefore, it is easily looked upon, not as a sign, but simply as another good cause (or, perhaps, misguided cause). Whenever the church has tried to compel faith—whether by force of law or simply through subtle intimidation—it has failed. But when the church understands its nature as *sign,* it has the power to nurture and strengthen faith and to be a community through which the life of God is offered to all.

To the church are given the signs we call sacraments. They are intended for the church, not for the world. This assertion indicates no mean or exclusive spirit. The gospel is offered to the world; the sacraments give the church the identity and strength to be a sign of the gospel in the world. The sacraments are not given directly to the world, and yet are given for the sake of the world.

Through baptism, God reminds the church of its identity; indeed, God imprints that identity upon it in order that the church may be the instrument of justice and righteousness in society. Jesus Christ thus gives to the church the commission set forth in Isaiah:

> Thus says God, the Lord,
>> who created the heavens and stretched them out,
>> who spread forth the earth and what comes from it,
>> who gives breath to the people upon it
>>> and spirit to those who walk in it;
> "I am the Lord, I have called you in righteousness,
>> I have taken you by the hand and kept you;
> I have given you as a covenant to the people,
>> a light to the nations,

to open the eyes that are blind,
to bring out the prisoners from the dungeon,
  from the prison those who sit in darkness.
I am the Lord; that is my name;
  my glory I give to no other,
  nor my praise to graven images.
Behold, the former things have come to pass,
  and new things I now declare;
before they spring forth I tell you of them."    (Isa. 42:5-9)

At the close of Matthew's Gospel, this divine imperative is brought into sharp focus, and is specifically related to baptism:

All authority in heaven and on earth has been given to me. Go therefore and make disciples of all nations, baptizing them in the name of the Father and of the Son and of the Holy Spirit, teaching them to observe all I have commanded you; and lo, I am with you always, to the close of the age.    (Matt. 28:18-20)

Jesus Christ, his church, and the sacraments, all are signs given in order for the sake of the whole creation.

The story communicated to us through baptism is given not for the purpose of information, but of incorporation: to make the church truly the body *(corpus)* of Christ in and for the world. As the formation of human personality rests upon the ability to remember one's identity, so it is through knowing who we are in God's sight that we become what we are intended to be. By the power of the Holy Spirit, Christ acts through baptism to form the church as his people, his body on earth. Because this activity is a divine mystery, no experience from other areas of life can illustrate it adequately; yet human experiences can help to clarify the power of ritual acts to establish identity.

Recently a news item told of Vietnamese refugee children who learned in their American school the stories of the Pilgrims and the customs of Thanksgiving. The children insisted that on a November Thursday the recently arrived family must eat turkey with all of the trimmings. Hardly a typical Vietnamese diet, we may suppose; yet the family complied and even wore pilgrim-type hats made from paper.

25

Why? Because through this action attached to a story, the heritage of the adopted land became their own. Thus it has been for generation upon generation of immigrants. Probably there are no Americans, regardless of ethnic background or recency of arrival, who do not in some sense own the Pilgrims as their ancestors. Through ritual activity connected to a story, a new identity is established.

Ritual action has the power to communicate and incorporate. That is how God has made us; and that is why God has given us sacraments—divine gifts designed to match a capacity put within us at creation. Baptism is not merely an audiovisual aid, soon forgotten. It is a sign that brings to pass, by the power of the Holy Spirit, the very identity it proclaims.

The sign is far more than a subjective experience. It is an objective act bound up with the faithful promise of God. That Christians experience deep personal feelings related to faith, there can be no doubt, but faith cannot rest on feelings. Otherwise, when we are in a happy mood we consider that God is good, loving, and gracious, but when depression overtakes us we begin to suspect that God is cold, distant, and stingy. The identity the Holy Spirit gives us is far more stable than that. To be baptized is to be incorporated into the God who is gracious whether we happen to feel like it on a certain day or not. When feelings fail, we can rely upon the sign and thus find strength.

Incorporation into Christ means not only that we are united with him, but that we are united with all who are in him. The body of believers is a corporate unity, not a conglomeration of individuals. Indeed, there is little sense of identity apart from multiple relationships. I am the husband of one woman, the son of another, and the father of two others. To many people, I am a teacher; to others, a former pastor; and to still more, a neighbor up the street. Without wife, mother, daughters, students, parishioners, and neighbors I could not know who I am in any complete sense. Likewise, Christians have no solid identity apart from community. This does not mean that Christian identity is not personal. The gospel is always personal, yet never individualistic. There is a crucial difference. Baptism is Christ's word addressed to us personally through the community of faith; it is his assurance that each of us is indeed included in his atoning, justifying act on behalf of the world.

When we understand it in this way, baptism can never again be viewed as simply an imitation of what Jesus of Nazareth experienced in the Jordan River under John the Baptizer. We are not called to be *like* Jesus (which we cannot fully be in any case); we are enabled to be *in* Jesus Christ by the power of the Holy Spirit. Once we grasp this, we will see as misguided the requests to be bapized in the Jordan, with water brought from that river, or simply under paintings or mosaics of that location. That is to settle for far too little. (It is worth noting that, despite the relative proximity of Jerusalem to the Jordan, there is no hint in the New Testament that the early church took anyone there, or brought water from that river for use in the rite.) God does not employ some special water, but through all water reveals that the whole of creation is a divine gift. God does not exhort us to imitate Jesus, but incorporates us into our Lord's full saving work.

In most denominations familiar to us, as the water is administered the minister says, "[NAME], I baptize you in the Name of the Father and of the Son of the Holy Spirit." This is a powerful assertion. Our names (that is, our whole identity, in the biblical understanding of things) are taken up into, united with, the ineffable Name of God. Frequently the Trinitarian baptismal formula is misunderstood to mean that God's name is "Father, Son, Holy Spirit." But a proper understanding of God's "name" is far more expansive than that. We can know much about God through the Trinitarian designation; but always beyond our ability to comprehend there is the God who is far greater than our minds, the God whose most sacred name is holy, separate, set off from all other names so as to be unspeakable. Probably the name which at the beginning of the Lord's Prayer is referred to as "hallowed" is the sacred name revealed to Moses [YAHWEH], which in Jesus' time was never uttered by devout Jews, who substituted another word in its place.

Thus in the baptismal formula we have an important theological contrast. Our names are openly stated there; for the God who receives us in baptism knows us fully. But God's holy name is only alluded to; for we cannot fully embrace divine mystery. Not only does God know us more fully that we can know God, but the Creator knows the creatures even more fully than we can know ourselves. True human identity is achieved, not through introspection, but through incorporation into the One whose mystery reveals and calls forth our hidden potential.

To the richness of this truth, the baptismal liturgy of the Eastern Orthodox churches adds another insight; for there the minister says "[NAME] is baptized in the Name of the Father and of the Son and of the Holy Spirit." What is implied is this: "[NAME] is baptized by Jesus Christ himself through the power of the Holy Spirit." Only Christ can incorporate us into his body; and this he does. Baptism is his act in the church. Only the One who has ascended on high can take our names and bring them into eternal unity with the mysterious Name of God. This is the Lord's doing; it is intended to be marvelous in our eyes.

# 2

# LIFE IN CHRIST:
# THE CHURCH'S RESPONSE

We have been looking at baptism from the divine side: The sacrament is God's gift, by means of which Jesus Christ incorporates us into a new covenant and a new creation; by the power of the Holy Spirit, we discover who we really are in relation to our Creator.

But what about human responsibility and participation in all of this? It may appear that if God does so much, there is little left for us to do. Then baptism becomes an automatic transaction that easily slips over into magic and superstition. To prevent such a distortion, we now must consider how God's gift in baptism is related to our repentance and faith, to our obedient service as Christian witnesses in the world.

## THE CHURCH AS COVENANT COMMUNITY

Usually discussion about the Christian life begins by talking about people as individuals and later looks at how these individuals interact. Thus, we assume that life in Christ begins with the conversion of particular people, who then voluntarily assemble themselves into an organization (the church) for reasons of practical efficiency and mutual support. But we will not understand the true nature of the Christian faith so long as we assume that the church is essentially an expendable society of like-minded individuals who decide to gather together to pursue common religous concerns.

The church is, instead, a community called into being at God's initiative. It is an essential assembly, without which those who come forth from the font are still-born. To those who have been reared on a doctrine of rugged individualism, such a statement may appear to be extreme; but its truth can be demonstrated.

Without the community of Israel, which produced prophets and teachers, Scripture and liturgy, there could have been no New Testament church. Without the church, not one of us would be alive in Christ today; for our faith is dependent upon Scripture and tradition.[1] Scripture is a unique witness to God's love in Jesus Christ; but it is a book written, transmitted, translated, and interpreted within the community of faith. Tradition is also dependent upon the community. Without the church, there would have been no councils to define doctrine, no passing on of collections of hymns and prayers, no continuity in preaching, teaching, and ethical inquiry and practice.

The church is God's creation and gift; it is within the church that we discover who we are in relation to God and one another. In our human society, we have what today we call the nuclear family (the nucleus consisting of parents and children) and the extended family (other relatives and even "adopted" family). So also in the family of Christ. The nuclear unit of the covenant is the parish congregation; it is essential to our life in Christ. Yet we cannot stop at this level and have an adequate base from which to work. There is also the extended community of the covenant, which the creeds refer to as the holy catholic church. In this extended family are not only parish congregations of every denomination across the whole earth, but also the entire company of believers in every age—that communion of saints that transcends distance and time.

Through baptism, we are made, and discover ourselves to be, the brothers and sisters of Peter and James and John; of Mary and Martha and Lazarus of Bethany; of Magdalene and Mary the mother of Jesus; of Ambrose, and of Monica and her son, Augustine; of Francis of Assisi and Claire, his disciple; of Luther and Calvin; of Susanna and Samuel Wesley and their renowned sons, John and Charles; of John XXIII and John Paul I; and of an almost infinite host of others whose names have been forgotten by us but not by God. The richness and insight and devotion we can draw upon within this extended family is indispensable as we seek to be the faithful followers of Christ. It is from within the community of the covenant that we respond to God.

## REPENTANCE AND FAITH

Those who experience the new life in Christ turn from sin and rebellion to trust in the righteousness and sufficiency of God. The relationship between the turning (which we call repentance) and the trusting (which we call faith) is not always adequately understood, however—primarily because our thinking is too sequential and individualistic in orientation.

Usually, we assume that first the individual must repent of sin, and then must live by faith. Yet the capacity for repentance itself presupposes at least some faith and action upon it. If we have no faith in the righteousness of God and no desire to live differently, then how can we turn—or why should we? Nor is repentance merely a momentary, introductory step; it is a continued about-face directed toward good. So bound together are these two elements that the entire life in Christ can properly be thought of as a life of repentance-faith.

In the New Testament, indications of the linkage of repentance and faith are numerous and varied. Particularly in the Synoptic Gospels, repentance is seen to be a radical turning that has the continuing effect of redirecting the whole of life into the eschatological kingdom of Christ. So seriously was this same total and continuing redirection taken in the Letter to the Hebrews that the restoration of those who had experienced, and then renounced it, was regarded as being impossible (Heb. 6:4–6). In Pauline writings, the term of repentance *(metanoia)* occurs infrequently, and in Johannine literature, not at all. This does not reflect a lack of importance attached to the new way of life but, rather, a holistic approach to repentance-faith—all faith is presumed to involve a turning from sin.[2]

The penitent-faithful church is committed to perpetual vigilance against sin and perpetual dedication to sanctification. It is not even sufficient to say that our life in Christ is one of repentance followed by faith, followed by sin and doubt, followed by renewed repentance and faith, with an endless repetition of this sequence. It is certain that we do sin again and again, and seek restoration. But the image we are to have of ourselves is not that of Sisyphus who struggles to push his rock to the top of the hill, only to be overpowered by it each time he almost reaches the summit. A theology of chronic back-sliding may be popular and comforting; but it is not sufficient for those who live in Christ and trust in the power of the Spirit to help them. In the Christian life, sin and sanctification may exist simultaneously but not sequentially. To understand this better we need to look more deeply at the origin and meaning of faith.

We must wrestle with a fundamental question: how do we come to the faith that characterizes God's covenant people? Having rejected the idea that repentance precedes and is merely a prelude to faith, we now question another common assumption—that faith is something we bring to the church, that it is something we somehow generate and then present to God. In difficult times, we may say to ourselves (or others), "Come on, now. Just have a little faith," as if faith were something we could produce by pushing the correct button. Such counsel is misleading, and can result in great spiritual frustration. Consider another approach.

In the Roman Catholic liturgical tradition, those who are coming for baptism are greeted at the door of the church with the question, "What do you ask of God's church?" The answer to be given is, "Faith." We may be inclined to think that the more appropriate question for this answer would be, "What do you bring to God's church?" But the traditional query has behind it a deep insight. To be sure, we do not come to baptism with a total lack of faith; but we come seeking an increase of faith, as did the man who came to Jesus saying, "Lord, I do believe. Help the little faith I have" (Mark 9:24, Jerusalem Bible).[5]

The role of the community in nurturing the faith of those within it becomes more evident when we look at the nature of faith itself. The distinction sometimes made between faith *in* (dependence upon God) and faith *that* (acceptance of doctrinal statements) deserves to be questioned. The two forms of faith are not easily separated. We come to trust *in* the reliability of God as we learn *that* Jesus, God's messiah, died for our sin, rose for our justification, works in us through the Spirit, and will rule over all unrighteousness. Without faith *that*, faith *in* becomes empty-headed emotionalism; without faith *in*, faith *that* becomes empty-hearted dogmatism. The two forms of faith interpenetrate each other.

Within the church, doctrinal reflection and practical trust with its ethical dimension belong together. The church's announcement of what God has done, is doing, and will yet do, motivates and empowers us to turn from sin to righteousness as those who already live in God's coming kingdom.

Furthermore, within the church we discover the communal basis of personal faith. Almost all of us who claim a living faith came to it through being reared in the church (even if we rebelled against the church for a time, or barely grasped the faith until late in life). Even those who had no early associations with a congregation and in maturity came to faith through reading or through the witness of friends or neighbors nevertheless received the gospel through the community. For those who wrote and those who testified did so from within the church. The covenant people from generation to generation pass on the tradition received from the apostles, and in the process act as a check against the aberrations of individuals and of the separatist movements the community spawns in moments of uncritical enthusiasm.

It is not uncommon in the history of the church to find that third and fourth generation adherents of a sectarian movement begin to resemble the church from which their forebears broke far more than they resemble the original break-away group itself. Cynics see this as a sign of capitulation to the status quo, which in some cases it may be; but in other instances, it is evidence that the community of faith as a whole exercises a restraining and correcting influence upon its maverick parts. Eventually the weaknesses inherent in an idiosyncratic faith become so manifest that the strength of the corporate wisdom and practice is seen to be preferable.

Within the church, we are challenged to respond to Christ's act in our baptism. We are free to react in a variety of ways. We may respond by being the grateful, obedient people of grace who live out the identity we have been given through the water of the sacrament; that is surely God's desire and hope for us. But we may instead respond by being lackadaisical or even contemptuous; every parish has on its roll of baptized persons a distressing number of those who prove this point. Baptism is not a mechanical or magical act that deprives us of our freedom to reject God's claim upon us. But neither is the power of God nullified when those who have been baptized refuse to live up to their calling.

If we are tempted to question the power of baptism because some of the baptized fail to understand their identity, that temptation is greatly lessened when we think corporately (about the role of the church) rather than individualistically (about the reaction of the uncommitted). For a faithful congregation of Christ's people seeks in every possible way to keep in touch with those who appear to have lost interest, urging them on and prodding them to be faithful to their covenant. Thus, the congregation responds faithfully to God, even though some of its members may not.

When the uncommitted do return to embrace their baptismal faith, even that return may be seen as a fruit of the sacrament. In the story of the prodigal son, the young man says to himself while in the far country, "I will arise and go to my father, and I will say to him, 'Father, I have sinned. . . .' " (Luke 15:18). Why does he say this rather than, "I will arise and go to a stranger, and I will say, 'Stranger, I have had a streak of bad luck' "? How does the prodigal know anything about a personal relationship? How does he know to differentiate between sin and tough luck? And what gives him the courage to assume responsibility for his own failure and future? Surely all of this is the result of his experience before he ventured into the far country. Before he left home, he was given an identity which he could not shake off even among pigs and corn husks. His repentance is nothing other than a decision to act positively, rather than rebelliously, with respect to that indelible identity.

In baptism, we are indelibly stamped with the identity Jesus Christ won for us through his Incarnation, death, and Resurrection. We can refuse to acknowledge our true identity. From our viewpoint, we can even renounce it and reject all of its benefits. Yet we cannot change it. We are what God has made us to be. We cannot prevent God from regarding us as

34

those who have been ransomed by divine love, from striving continually to bring us to our senses, and from running out to greet us at the first indication of our return. Nor can we prevent God from trying to woo us through the ministry of the church, and from reintroducing us into its community when we respond. Even the repentance of the wayward baptized, when it comes, is made possible by the faithfulness of God, signified in baptism and proclaimed by the church. Faith is never a work; always it is the gift of God.

## OBEDIENT SERVICE IN THE WORLD

God's gift of faith bears fruit in obedient service. Obedience and service are not popular words in our age (or in any age, likely). Obedience often seems to mean blind acquiescence or compliance under constraint. Service, while less distasteful, when coupled with the word *obedient* may conjure up visions of servile passivity to the whims of a dictator. None of these interpretations expresses the Christian understanding of that which flows from faith.

Baptism enables us to have a changed perception of what it means to be obedient servants of the Lord. The God who gives us the sacrament as a means of self-revelation is sovereign, but is not an arbitrary autocrat. Therefore, we are not the dehumanized subjects of a celestial tyrant. Through baptism, we are incorporated into Jesus Christ, and confess that he is Lord. But the term *Lord Jesus Christ* is to be understood in its totality. Jesus came as servant of all, and was the Incarnation of love. As if to stress the difference between his lordship and that of feudal rulers, John's Gospel reports to us an occasion on which Jesus told his followers, "No longer do I call you servants, for the servant does not know what his master is doing; but I have called you friends" (John 15:15). It was in this context of redefined terms that Jesus gave his followers the commendment to love (John 15:9-14).

We who are baptized into Christ do not obey God because we fear the consequences if we do otherwise. Nor do we serve in the hope of winning divine favor and thus gaining admission into God's kingdom. Baptism reminds us that we are saved by grace, not by works, and that we already are citizens of the kingdom. Baptism proclaims divine love and thereby causes love to spring forth within us: "We love because God first loved us" (I John 4:19).

St. Theresa reported a dream in which she saw a woman running with great purpose, carrying in one hand a torch and in the other a pail of water. Theresa inquired of her where she was going, and the woman replied, "I am going to quench the fires of hell and burn down the mansions of heaven so that people will love God for God's own sake, not because they fear punishment or seek reward." Perhaps it is not pressing things too much to suggest that the water of baptism and the fire of the Holy Spirit given to us through the sacrament should serve the purpose within us revealed to Theresa in her dream.

The love that makes us obedient servants is active—a driving force, not a static experience. A currently popular bumper sticker advises us that "Christians aren't perfect—just forgiven." This is remarkably close to the truth, and yet perilously far from it. The slogan might more properly read: "Christians aren't perfect—just forgiven and pressing on toward perfection." But even that revision is inadequate; for sanctification is not to be confused with sheer determination. The truth is that we are propelled and empowered by the Holy Spirit, who continually prods and points the way.

In order to understand better what our obedient service looks like in practical terms, we draw one example from the world of nature, one from the social order, and one from the life of the church itself.

The close relationship between the sacraments and the created order has implications concerning our regard for and use of the natural world. A despoiled creation is a broken instrument in the hand of God, more of a hindrance to divine self-communication than a means of it. Therefore, the church as obedient servant seeks to exercise a responsible concern for the natural order. The Christian vision of the sanctity of the earth goes beyond the common assumptions made in the name of ecology alone. Appeals to clean up the water and air, conserve depletable resources, and protect the flora and fauna frequently rest upon self-interest (we will suffer if we do not change our ways), and upon the assumption that creation exists entirely for human benefit. A Christian understanding of God's work sees creation as being valuable in itself, apart from whatever benefits we may derive from it. Our view of the world as sacramental gives us a sense of urgency about restoring creation to the splendor and fullness God gave it. The grace announced to us through the sacraments provides the proper motivation: we act not out of guilt or selfishness, but from gratitude and an assurance that we work in the power of the Spirit.

Baptism also gives us a vision of a new social order. All of us come to baptism as sinners equally guilty before God, and all of us come away from baptism as those who have been made God's adopted sons and daughters through grace. Once we grasp this, any supposed superiority based on race, social class, gender, or nationality is exposed as a lie. Furthermore, those who through baptism are made to recognize their equality seek a society in which all receive justice, in which all share as members of a common family under God. Opportunism and suppression of the rights of others are contrary to the meaning of baptism. Therefore, those who are already citizens of the coming kingdom renounce false values and methods; they seek to make life in this world conformable to life in God's eternal kingdom. That is the meaning of the unceasing petition of the baptized: "Thy kingdom come . . . on earth as it is in heaven."

Christians may disagree about the best social models to follow and about the most effective means of achieving the goals, but the company of the baptized cannot brook fundamental disagreement about the pursuit of a social order in which all persons are granted full rights, opportunities, and responsibilities. Neither can the baptized naïvely pursue a utopia achievable by zeal and good intentions. Christians know the extent of sin just as they know the power of grace; within the tension of these two forces a realistic understanding of social progress must be fashioned. Therefore, both the possibilities and the limitations of economic and political processes must be faced candidly.

As baptism gives us a new view of the natural order and the social order, so the sacrament also provides us with a new vision of the church itself. According to Scripture, there is "one body and one Spirit, . . . one hope, . . . one Lord, one faith, one baptism" (Eph. 4:4-6). This fact challenges the internal divisions of the Christian community. The church may well affirm, as the Ephesian letter goes on to do, that grace has been imparted differently according to the measure of Christ's gift; therefore, to require of Christians an absolute uniformity is contrary to true unity. But that is not to condone, let alone to encourage, pride of separation based upon forms of church government, ethnic origin, or variation in doctrine on matters that are not of first-rank importance. Certainly it is not to bless rivalry between denominations or the misrepresentation of one group by another. To be bapized and not to agonize over ecclesiastical division, not to work toward the unity of the church, is a contradiction in terms. At the same time, to confuse unity with uniformity is to fail to understand that baptism creates a community capable of embracing different expressions of a common faith and witness.

Within the new vision of the church we find clues about how to handle the tension that often exists between the call to unity and the call to righteousness. What, for example, shall the church say about war? Shall Christians oppose all war as being contrary to the will of God? Or shall we support wars selectively, on the assumption that some of them can be just? Or shall we support all wars that are legally declared, on the ground that we are to submit to governmental authorities as having been constituted by God? All three positions have been held by sincere Christians. Or consider a question whose answers more closely follow denominational lines: shall abortion be condemned absolutely as murder, or allowed as being under certain circumstances an affirmation of the dignity of life? If the church cannot agree on questions such as these, then is it not prudent to keep silent in order to maintain the unity of the church?

Our baptism, which calls us to unity, also calls us to righteousness, not to neutrality. We are not to pursue one call to the exclusion of the other. Because of the identity Christ gives us in baptism, we can hold different ideas about what constitutes righteousness in practical terms while recognizing one another as brothers and sisters within God's family.

Recall our revised bumper sticker: "Christians aren't perfect; just forgiven and pressing on toward perfection." The fact that we cannot agree in all things is an obvious evidence that we are not perfect. The ability to disagree without being divided can be a testimony that the forgiveness we have experienced is a transforming power, not merely a celestial transaction. The determination to take a stand on the basis of the best we know, while at the same time seeking further understanding, can be evidence of our drive toward perfection. Thus, we can be what Christ intends the church to be—a sign to the world. But the term *world* has two quite different meanings in Scripture; in order to understand our role, we need to untangle these two strands.

On the one hand, the term *world* has a very positive meaning. The world is God's creation. Jesus Christ has come into the world for the sake of the world. But the term has a negative connotation also. Frequently Christians have lumped together "the world, the flesh, and the devil." The ambiguity is evident in the New Testament itself, particularly within John's Gospel. There it is said that "God so loved the world that he gave his only Son" (John 3:16; see also John 1:29; 8:12; and 12:46-47). Yet it is asserted that the Lord's disciples are "not of the world" but have been chosen out of the world (John 15:19; see also John 7:7; 12:31; 14:17; and 17:14).[4] What are we to make of this?

The world, when spoken of in a positive sense, has to do with God's activity and the human response of faith; the negative sense of the term pertains to all that is rebellious and contrary to God's intention. Both of these realities dwell together in a creation that has fallen into sin, as baptism makes clear. We are called to witness to the grace of God in order that the disobedient world may become what God intends it to be. New life in Christ is not an other-worldly existence that produces ecclesiastical isolationism or spiritual nose-thumbing. Our enmity is against sin in the world, not against creation itself.

We, the baptized people of God, are to be what God intends the world to become. By virtue of our incorporation into Christ we have a priestly work to do. Under the ministry of Jesus Christ, the great high priest, all Christians offer to God the joys and concerns of the world, all pray and make offerings on behalf of the world. Thus God is pleased to use the church as a sign: "We are ambassadors for Christ, God making his appeal through us" (II Cor. 5:20). It is the joy of the church to be God's obedient servant that the world may believe.

The community of repentance and faith responds to the baptismal covenant by praying continually that the Spirit may work unhampered. For the church knows that without the Spirit's ministry it is exactly what the world is all too likely to mistake it for being—just another human institution, one voluntary organization along side of, and on the same plane as, many others. But through the power of the Spirit, the church can be a harbinger to the world of what God wills the world to be: Christ's new creation made alive by the gift of divine grace.

Everything that the penitent-faithful community does is a response to that same grace, a working-out of the identity Christ has given us in baptism. And so the church makes common confession with Paul that we have not already obtained perfection; but we press on to make it our own, because Christ Jesus has made us his own (Phil. 3:12).

# 3

# THE WHO'S WHO
# OF BAPTISM

We come now to specific matters that often raise perplexing questions about baptism. Who are the proper candidates for baptism? Who constitute special cases: emergency baptism, baptism of the retarded and the senile, baptism "in the name of Jesus only," "spiritual baptists" such as members of the Society of Friends and the Salvation Army, requests for rites of "infant dedication"? Then we must ask, "Who are the proper ministers of baptism?" Finally there is the persistent and problematic question, "Is baptism necessary for salvation?"

## WHO SHALL BE BAPTIZED?

The variety of possible answers to the question concerning proper candidates for baptism is bounded on the one side by the inclusive position and on the other by the exclusive position. The inclusive view is that virtually all who request the rite for themselves or their children are to be admitted. This was the posture of pre-reformation Europe such that, at times, military leaders could virtually order the "conversion" of peoples they had conquered. In less extreme form, the inclusive answer is still dominant among the state churches on the continent and in Britain, but is not limited to them. The exclusive view is that baptism is only for those who make a conscious profession of faith. Thus, persons below a certain age are excluded, as are adults who make no clear articulation of faith. This was the posture of the Anabaptists at the time of the Reformation and of their spiritual descendants. It is a view held by some persons in almost every denomination today,

41

including the churches that officially hold to the inclusive concept, or something close to it.

The concept of baptism as a rite open to all within the Christian sphere of influence views the church as a creation of God, and sees baptism as being an action of Christ within the church. Baptism is regarded as having an objective character, and is offered to all because God has offered the grace of the gospel to all. Persons are welcomed into the family of God even if they are young in years or faith. The strengths of the inclusive position are its emphases upon divine initiative, objectivity, and the all-embracing nature of Christ's family.

The inclusive view has grave weaknesses, however. Stress upon the sacramental character of baptism can lead to misunderstanding so that the rite comes to be viewed mechanically, or even magically. In the worst distortions, baptism is considered a kind of escape hatch from perdition or a guarantee of salvation. It may appear that nothing is required with respect to commitment or growth; thus the church becomes an institution that lacks discipline. In the countries that have state churches, the problem is compounded; those who pay taxes to support the church expect its services without question. Thus, the church becomes the servant of the state, or of popular sentiment, at least. Furthermore, the line between national citizenship and citizenship in the kingdom of God becomes excessively blurred.

The exclusive view has its strengths precisely at the points of weakness in the inclusive position. Baptism as an exclusive rite demands adult commitment, and can never be seen as a mechanical transmission of grace to be granted indiscriminately. Churches that hold the exclusive position seek to be intentional fellowships of articulated faith and active Christian life. In countries with state churches, the exclusive groups are generally small, vigorous, and highly disciplined. Because in some cases their members must support the state church through taxes and the non-state church through voluntary contributions, those who elect to belong to the non-state groups exhibit a level of commitment that is rarely found in inclusive churches.

The exclusive understanding of baptism also brings with it

a set of weaknesses, however. Usually baptism is not seen as God's activity, except to the extent that all things are under divine direction. To be sure, baptism was instituted by Christ, and thus is an order (or ordinance) to be obeyed. But popularly, at least, baptism is more likely regarded as a reward for faith than as a means of grace.[1] The church so constituted is not so much the creation of Christ as it is the voluntary association of those who profess faith. Such a church then tends to view faith either as verbal articulation of doctrine, or as personal testimony to a religious experience (usually called conversion). Thus, the church easily becomes a clique either of the like-minded, or of the like-hearted. Those who hold variant doctrines, or who have had dissimilar experiences, are at least suspect, and may even be regarded as being outside the pale of salvation.

The extreme inclusive position rests upon the divine side of the covenant. God's action is crucial; human response, while never called unimportant, is often under-emphasized. The extreme exclusive position proceeds from the opposite side of the covenant. Contemporary response to God is of the essence while the objectivity of Christ's saving work is frequently obscured, and attention is focused upon the individual rather than the community. A symptom of this is found in expressions many use in reporting their religious experiences ("I found Jesus"; "I accepted the Lord"), and in the recent bumper-sticker declaration, "I found it." A rejoinder used by some of the Jewish faith announces, "We never lost it." The change of pronouns reveals the weakness of Christian individualism, but both sides of the bumper-sticker game miss the point that God is not an "it," and that we are not the initiators of the experience of faith. A helpful corrective is found in the neglected hymn text:

> I sought the Lord and afterward I knew
> He moved my soul to seek him, seeking me;
> It was not I that found, O Savior true;
> No, I was found of thee.

The sentiment is still individualistic, but it corrects basic deficiencies in the ultra-exclusive expression of faith.

Among Protestants in the United States, the exclusive and inclusive positions do not generally exist in polarized form. While some inclusive churches may accept all candidates who make even the slightest pretense of faith, most parishes are less lenient; in the case of infants, for example, they require that at least one parent be a committed Christian who can be counted on to take responsibility for the nurture of the child. In the case of adult candidates, usually some form of pre-baptismal program (inquirer's class or individual consultation with the pastor) is assumed. Nor is the exclusive principle rigidly enforced in many quarters where it is officially held. It is evident, for example, that such churches administer baptism in many instances to persons so young that by any reasonable standard they cannot be called mature, responsible believers.[2] Nor is there any effective way to identify and reject youth and adults who present themselves for baptism because of peer pressure or social convention, rather than because of deep commitment.

Given the fact that most Protestants in this country fall between the extremes, we need to face this question: is the extreme toward which we tend such an inviolate ideal that we should feel guilty for not attaining it; or is it possible that the Holy Spirit is trying to tell us something about the folly of absolutistic stances? Experience, after all, is a worthy contributor in theological formulation. Perhaps the experience that none of us seems willing, let alone able, to hold to the extreme is a divine nudge in the direction of looking at baptism in a more whole way. Perhaps there is a middle way, which, instead of being a weak compromise, is a healthy resolution.

To the question, "Who shall be baptized?" we therefore suggest an answer that avoids the polarities, yet incorporates the concerns of both positions and adds one concern often overlooked by them: baptism is to be granted *to those who are committed to the Christian faith and to their children, provided they have not been baptized before.* This answer now deserves detailed explication.

Baptism is *for the committed.* Commitment is an elusive quality. Who does the judging, and on what basis? The difficulty is that there seems to be no less slippery way of avoiding the excesses to which the exclusive position can take us than to use the term *commitment*. To suggest instead that baptism is for those who have faith, presents still worse difficulties and perils for those who must judge. The familiar requirement of the exclusive churches that candidates be able to comprehend and articulate the faith raises yet thornier problems. What is faith? How can one distinguish between faith that is adequate and faith that is marginal or worse? What constitutes good comprehension and articulation? If commitment is not the perfect standard, at least it has a competitive edge over other contenders.

Commitment inescapably pertains to community. Those who seek baptism renounce by word and action the popular attitude, "I can be a committed Christian without being a member of the church." Harsh as this judgment may seem, we must hold that baptism is not intended for such people. Through baptism, Christ creates the church, both local and catholic. We can no more be baptized and avoid participation in the community than water can be boiled without becoming steam.

How commitment sufficient for baptism is determined is a matter with which each congregation and generation has to wrestle. To give neat and timeless formulae is to invite a legalism that defeats the entire enterprise. But the fact that commitment to the faith and the community of Christ is necessary for baptized Christians should be a matter beyond debate. The indiscriminate administration of the sacrament is at the least a misguided practice; and given the serious nature of God's covenant with us, perhaps it is not too much to call indiscriminate baptism a serious sin. For the church that allows it has not taken seriously the implications of the identity Christ gives us through baptism.

Having adopted the emphasis upon commitment which is the strength of the exclusive churches, now we adopt the emphasis upon dynamic inter-relatedness in the family of Christ which is the strength of the inclusive bodies. Baptism is for those who are committed to the Christian faith *and for their children*. In unusual cases definitions may be broadened somewhat. For example, parents may freely confess that they are not committed and do not wish to take the vows concerning their children under false pretenses, for which they should be commended. However, they may have no objection to having their children raised within the church and may, in fact, look favorably upon having relatives or friends assume the responsibility for this nurture. Such cases are relatively rare but have been known to have happy results—including the ultimate conversion of the parents, in some cases. Not every infant, however, is automatically a candidate for baptism; still less should infants be baptized as a missionary gesture toward the parents. Therefore, to avoid misunderstanding about who are included as children of the covenant, we need to look at the theological basis for the baptism of persons regardless of age.

The baptism of infants and children rests upon two great pillars, either of which is incapable of supporting the practice without the other. One pillar is the conviction that God's grace goes ahead of us, preparing the way of faith. (Technically this is called "prevenient grace" from the Latin *prae-*, before, and *venire*, to come.) God does not wait for us to request help or even to know that we need it. This is the understanding of divine goodness put forth by Paul: "While we were yet helpless, at the right time Christ died for the ungodly. Why, one will hardly dare to die for a righteous man. . . . But God shows his love for us in that while we were yet sinners Christ died for us" (Rom. 5:6-8). The same insight is found in I John 4:19: "We love, because God first loved us."

But if baptism rested on this pillar alone, we would be obliged to go about the world baptizing every youngster, whether the child of Christians, Hindus, Muslims, or atheists. Baptism speaks of God's initiating love which places us within the sphere of the community of faith in Christ. Thus, the second great pillar upon which the baptism of children rests is the corporate nature of our faith and the relation of the Holy Spirit to the body of believers created by Christ through the sacrament. Baptism, at whatever age it is administered, is not an incantation that operates automatically, but is our initiation into the covenant community. Under the power and direction of the Spirit, the church nurtures and disciplines those who are thus made a part of it.

The Old Testament understanding of the covenant did not admit distinctions on the basis of age. Children were brought into the covenant by virtue of the fact that God's promises were given to Noah's family and their descendants, to Abraham and Sarah and their descendants, to the Hebrew slaves released from Egypt and their descendants unto every generation. Peter's sermon the Day of Pentecost (by means of which Luke set forth his understanding of the nature of the church) took up this theme. Peter declared: "The promise is to you and to your children and to all that are far off, every one whom the Lord our God calls to him" (Acts 2:39). Hence the assumption that the church is for adults only is a strange one.

Then why is it that the New Testament makes no specific mention of the baptism of infants or children? Two answers are given so frequently that it is unnecessary to mention them, except in order to point out their weaknesses. First, it is suggested that most likely children were included in the household baptisms reported in Acts 11:14, 16:15, 18:8, and I Corinthians 1:16. But such a conjecture is shaky at best, and should not be relied upon. This matter sparked a lively, but inconclusive, debate among European theologians in the middle of this century. Karl Barth objected to the baptism of infants in light of the New Testament silence on the matter; but Oscar Cullmann rejected Barth's interpretation, and Joachim Jeremias produced what he considered to be evidence sufficient to prove a very early practice of baptizing children. Finally Kurt Aland said, in effect, " 'No' to all of the above"; against Cullmann and Jeremias, he argued that the baptism of infants is not warranted by clear biblical mandate or precedent; and against Barth, he argued that the baptism of infants is to be maintained in the church on broader biblical and doctrinal grounds.[3]

The desire to find New Testament warrant for the baptism of infants has resulted in exegetical violence. Appeal has been made, for example, to Jesus' words about becoming as little children and about receiving a child in his name (Mark 9:33-37 and parallels). These words may tell us something crucial about what is to characterize those who enter the kingdom, and thus indirectly they inform our understanding of baptism and discipleship; but in no way can these words be taken as biblical mandates for the baptism of children. Nor can Mark 10:13-16 and parallels ("let the children come") be responsibly so used, despite frequent inclusion in baptismal liturgies, hymns, and sermons. The mention of the "holy children" in I Corinthians 7:14 certainly suggests that the children of a believer are within the sphere of God's covenant grace; but again, this is not to say that children were baptized at Corinth, or anywhere else, in New Testament times.

Those who wish to deal responsibly with Scripture therefore suggest a second solution to New Testament silence: while the New Testament does not mandate the baptism of infants, neither does it forbid it. This suggestion readily suggests that we must choose between two competing principles: (a) what Scripture does not command, the church is forbidden to practice; (b) what Scripture does not forbid, the church is free to practice. The polarization of these positions, and the forced choice between them, has had unfortunate consequences historically. All parties in the debate need to face honestly the fact that on this issue the New Testament is of less help than we might wish. Kurt Aland was right: the decision about who may be proper candidates rests upon a broad base of biblical and historical theology, not upon a few carefully chosen passages of Scripture, nor upon an argument from silence.

What we can say with certainty is this: Based upon the New Testament evidence as a whole and upon the practice of the church in subsequent centuries, it is clear that children cannot be baptized until there exists a covenant community of adults in which these children can be nurtured. To put it formally: The baptism of adults is the norm; the baptism of children is derivative. This is not a quantitative matter; we do not mean that infants can be baptized only so long as a larger number of adults is baptized at the same time. But we do mean that the baptism of adults proclaims most fully what is implied in all baptism and that until a vital community of committed believers exists, one cannot go about baptizing children. This is obvious in any missionary situation (which is in effect what existed in New Testament times, and which may account for the New Testament's silence on the issue).

Experience makes it clear that once a community of committed adults does exist, questions about the status of their children will arise. Parents will be reluctant to regard their children merely as quasi-members of the covenant, and will reject entirely the suggestion that their children are heathen and must stand outside looking in until they reach a certain age. Thus some kind of liturgical action will almost inevitably arise as a way of dealing with the question, "Who are our children in relation to who we are before God?" It is hardly surprising, therefore, that children have come to be included in the act of baptism, once the community of committed adults has been formed.[4]

Baptism is for those committed to the Christian faith and community, and for their children. This presses upon the church the necessity of being what the church is intended to be: a family of Christ's people who discipline, nurture, and encourage one another in the faith. Neither adults nor children come to baptism complete; for all of us, it is a beginning point, not a destination. All approach the sacrament as those who are to be born anew; having been born, God's people are expected to grow. The more mature members of the community accept responsibility for helping the new Christians to increase in faithful obedience; but at the same time, the mature members expect to learn from, and to be aided in, their own growth by the new members. The assumption sometimes made that infants in the faith (whether children or adults chronologically) have little to contribute to the rest of the community is an inappropriate form of arrogance from a baptismal perspective. To all whom he incorporates into the church, Jesus Christ grants gifts by the power of the Holy Spirit. While these gifts may vary, all are necessary and complementary within the life of the family of God.

The statement concerning who may be baptized ends with a provision that may seem odd or unnecessary: "those who are committed to the Christian faith and to their children, *provided they have not been baptized before.*" Would that the facts warranted the deletion of that proviso, but the evidence is strongly on the other side. Almost all pastors receive requests for rebaptism; some accede to such requests, even defending their action vociferously.[5] Therefore, we need to look at why the provision is included.

The church has consistently stood fast against the practice of rebaptism. Even when the rite has been repeated, it has been because in the judgment of those who administered the water the second time, the first administration was not a true baptism; thus the later event was understood as the first baptism. The conundrum of rebaptism is ancient. In the third century, conflict arose over admission into the catholic church of those who claimed baptism by the schismatic Novations. Stephen, Bishop of Rome, held that the grace of Christ is effective no matter who performs the rite; therefore, penitent schismatics were to be received after only a rite of reconciliation. Cyprian of Carthage argued that no baptism performed by schismatics could be considered true baptism. Despite their divergent conclusions, both men started from the same premise: Rebaptism is impossible. One must decide whether what happened before was a true baptism, and then proceed accordingly.

In A.D. 314, the Synod of Arles ruled that those baptized at the hands of heretics should be questioned about their orthodoxy. Those affirming the catholic Trinitarian faith should be received with simply the laying on of hands as a sign of reconciliation. Others should be regarded as heretics still. There was to be no rebaptism. The conflict between the Donatists and Augustine also centered on the issue of rebaptism. The Donatists asserted that an alleged baptism performed by an immoral priest is not baptism at all. Augustine, following Arles, held that the sacraments are not dependent upon the minister.

Although the Anabaptists received their name because, in the view of others, they baptized again, these left-wing reformers themselves argued that they were administering baptism for the first time to each person, for the rite administered in infancy constituted no baptism at all. Contemporary Baptists take the same position, for the most part.

So strong has been the objection to rebaptism that a form for conditional baptism was devised for use when doubt existed as to whether a person had been baptized. In such cases this formula was used: "If you are not already baptized, I baptize you. . . ."

Why this emphasis on the unrepeatability of baptism? The answer lies in the conviction that the sacrament involves the action of God. Baptism is God's firm and steadfast covenant promise. Thus, to rebaptize is to say, "God, you once promised your steadfast love and creative power to this person. But perhaps you didn't mean it. Promise it again. You supposedly incorporated this person into the community of the covenant; perhaps that didn't take effect. Do it again." Hence, rebaptism impugns the integrity of God. Stated bluntly, rebaptism is a form of blasphemy—or else it is a way of saying that baptism doesn't mean anything at all in terms of divine activity. Either God can be counted upon to act, or baptism is simply a repeatable human gesture: a request to God, but not a declaration from God; an enacted affirmation or prayer, but not a sacramental gift to us.

Furthermore, while baptism is more than initiation in the secular sense, it is at least that much. Any organization that has initiation ceremonies would be perplexed if a member of some years came saying, "I want to be initiated again, please." The request seems to carry at its heart a failure to understand the meaning of words. It is impossible to be initiated into an organization more than once, just as it is impossible to be born into the physical world more than one time.[6]

Those who request rebaptism do not see it in this light, of course. They come for a variety of reasons. Some regard their baptism as being defective because of the denomination in which it was administered, or the age at which it occurred, or the manner in which the water was applied. Others simply have a low view of baptism and do not sense its indelible nature; they regard it as a repeatable rite that can be employed to produce a certain kind of religious experience or to mark a new stage of spiritual development. We shall look at these motivations separately in order to suggest ways in which to respond to each.

The case dealt with most easily arises from a belief that baptism is merely a mark of denominational identification. Someone comes saying, "I was baptized a Presbyterian, but I have married a Lutheran, and want to be baptized a Lutheran." Usually the matter can be resolved with a simple explanation that among the denominations that recognize baptism as a sacrament (including Roman Catholic, Lutheran, Episcopalian, Presbyterian, Methodist, and United Church of Christ bodies), baptism with water in the Name of the Father and of the Son and of the Holy Spirit is mutually accepted. The occasional disregard of this principle proves the rule. A celebrated instance occurred when then President Lyndon Johnson's daugher, Luci, was rebaptized prior to marrying a Roman Catholic. The late James Pike, a bishop of the Episcopal Church, in which she had been baptized, challenged the baptism. The Roman Church was gravely embarrassed by the improper action of one of its priests; that furor stands as a warning to any who might carelessly disregard the principle of mutual recognition of baptism.

While some non-sacramental churches do not recognize the baptism of the sacramental churches, the reverse is not true. For example, a Baptist wishing to join an Episcopal congregation would not be rebaptized, even though an Episcopalian going in the other direction would likely be required to submit to baptism again. The situation is changing, however; The Christian Church (Disciples), for example, will baptize only adults, and then by immersion. But it is the official policy of that denomination to accept by transfer baptized persons from other denominations, regardless of the mode of baptism used or the age at which it was administered. Many Baptists are moving in a similar direction.[7]

Nevertheless, the second category of requests for rebaptism will come from people who are dissatisfied because they were baptized at an early age. Often they will indicate that they have not *really* been baptized. A variant goes as follows: "I was baptized as a teenager [or, as a young adult], but I didn't really know what I was doing then. Now I have had a genuine experience of the Lord, and am ready to be really baptized." In such cases there is a failure to see baptism as God's action, from which later spiritual development and experience proceed. The concept of baptism as a promise that extends into the future is missing, as is the understanding that, by definition, we can be initiated only once. Still another variation on the same theme springs from semantic confusion. Someone will say: "I was christened as an infant. Now that I am grown up I want to be baptized." Here we have an assumption that christening and baptism are two different rites, distinguished by the age of the recipient, the manner in which the water is applied, or both. In fact, no such differentiation exists from a historical or theological perspective.

Because there is, however, a popular distinction between *christening* and *baptism*, particularly in certain geographical areas, it would be best for the church to abolish the word *christen* from its vocabulary. The uncertain etymology of the term has probably helped to create the confusion. The English word may be derived from the Greek term for the anointing oil (chrism) or from the new garment (crisome) given in certain rites. Or, *christen* may be the corruption of the English word *Christianize*. The confusion has been compounded through references to christening ships and other objects. Perhaps it is easier to abolish the troublesome term than to convince people that a christening is identical with a baptism.

People who are troubled because they think their baptism occurred at an age too early to be effective need to be helped to understand the importance of the faithfulness of God's promise and the ongoing nature of the covenant we enter into at baptism. In many instances, the requests for rebaptism because of age may be satisfied through a rite of the renewal or reaffirmation of the baptismal covenant, a matter discussed at more length in the next chapter.

A third group of requests for rebaptism will come from those who believe that the water must be administered in a certain way, for this way alone is biblical. A person will say: "I was baptized by pouring [or sprinkling]; but I want to be really baptized—the way Jesus was." What is being requested is baptism by submersion (immersion). Incredible as it will seem to those who make this request, there is no solid evidence in the New Testament concerning how Jesus, or anyone else, was baptized. Moreover, the assumption that submersion was *the only* New Testament mode is even more questionable than the assumption that it was *a* New Testament practice.

The pertinent passages in the New Testament indicate that those being baptized went down into the water, or came up out of it; this does not preclude the possibility that they simply stood in the water waist-deep or so, and had water poured over them, or washed themselves in it. These popular methods of ritual purification in pre-Christian circles appear in ancient Christian iconography. When the church got around to building baptismal pools instead of using streams, some of these baptistries seem to have been designed for a standing, rather than a supine, position; some of them featured a spout from which water flowed into the pool, so that even the early liturgies that refer to placing the head of the candidate under the water may refer to holding the head under the spout of flowing water, shower-bath fashion, rather than to submerging the head under the water in which the candidate stood.[8]

New Testament imagery about being buried with Christ in baptism (Rom. 6:4; Col. 2:12) is frequently offered as evidence of immersion as a New Testament practice. But this is not incontestable, either. First, there is a chicken-egg problem: did these passages presuppose a particular form, or were they instead referring to a meaning of baptism (death to the old age, resurrection into a new age) which quite legitimately gave rise to the form? Second, if these pasages in Romans and Colossians are taken literally, why is not this passage taken literally to mean that at Corinth baptism was administered by having the candidate drink a cup of water: "For by one Spirit we were all baptized into one body . . . and all were made to drink of one Spirit" (I Cor. 12:13)? Finally, as we shall see in more detail in chapter 5, baptism in the early centuries (and probably as early as New Testament times) was administered primarily at Easter. Therefore the passages in Romans and Colossians may allude to the timing, rather than to the manner, of baptism, when they speak of being buried and raised with Christ.

The plain and frustrating truth is that nothing in the New Testament tells us unambiguously in what way, or ways, baptism was administered. We do know from the *Didache* that, by about A.D. 100, provision existed for pouring water over the candidate; and around A.D. 256, Cyprian mentions baptism by sprinkling in the case of candidates who were seriously ill or confined to bed. That is not much help, but at least it indicates that these modes, which are commonly used today, are not recent innovations.

In any event, three modes of baptism have prevailed in the church. Each is acceptable in view of the fact that God's promise and grace are not dependent upon the amount of water or how it is applied, but upon the steadfastness of the promise attached to the water. No one baptized by any of these modes needs to be troubled. In the final chapter of this book, we will point out that some modes are more demonstrative of the judgment and grace proclaimed through the sacrament than are others, but this does not mean that God's action is dependent upon the manner in which the water is administered.

A fourth group of people will request rebaptism simply on the assumption that baptism is repeatable by nature. For some, a second baptism (or a third, or a fourth) simply marks a new stage of spiritual development. One man reported to me with some degree of pride that he had been baptized three times during adulthood, because twice he had back-slid and been restored. In such a view, baptism is simply a human confession of faith, not a sign of God's faithful promise, which persists despite our infidelity. Others who regard baptism as a repeatable rite see in it the source of a particular kind of religious feeling: baptism conveys a sense of joy or release at the moment of its administration. In fact, among those who hold this view, baptism may produce the desired effect simply because suggestion can readily give rise to all kinds of states of mind; but we should be wary of equating the power of suggestion with the power of the Holy Spirit.

Of all the requests for rebaptism, the last mentioned is the one to which clergy seem to accede most readily, particularly in the more evangelical wing of Protestantism; yet it is fraught with problems even from an evangelical perspective. Thoughtful evangelicals acknowledge the value of good feelings in connection with Christian commitment; but they understand that valid feelings are not produced by formula, whether the formula involves baptism or some other supposedly sure-fire technique. They also know that feelings are notoriously unreliable gauges of divine truth and love. When good feelings confirm our trust in the justice and mercy of God, all is well. But when such feelings fail, are we to suppose that God has suddenly become inactive or unreliable?

The people who have had the deepest Christian experiences seem to be the very ones who are most wary of relying upon emotions rather than upon the steadfastness of God in the midst of our changing moods. John Wesley reported that immediately following his Aldersgate experience "it was not long before the enemy suggested, 'This cannot be faith, for where is thy joy?' Then I was taught that 'peace and victory over sin are essential to faith in the Captain of our salvation but that, as to the transports of joy— that usually attend the beginning of it especially in those who have mourned deeply—God sometimes giveth, sometimes withholdest them, according to the counsel of his own will."[9]

It is one of the virtues of the sacraments that they offer us an objective assurance of God's love in those times when subjective indications fail us. To reduce the sacraments to an occasion for subjective experience is to discard one of the most valuable resources we have in times of spiritual dimness, difficulty, and doubt. We can learn much from the habit of Martin Luther who, in moments of discouragement, found strength in the words, "I am baptized." To grant requests for rebaptism to those who hope for a momentary spiritual uplift thereby is short-sighted. A deep and abiding assurance is exchanged for an uncertain and transitory experience. This fact should be emphasized to those who request rebaptism because they believe it will have a happy effect upon them at the moment of its administration.

Regardless of why requests for rebaptism come, acquiescence to them makes the sacrament less and less a divine gift of unique import and dependability, and more and more a mere human invention subject to our rules and whims. This the church has come to understand through long and painful experience; it is a lesson we ignore at our peril. Prevention, of course, is far more effective than attempted cures. Once people are convinced that they need to be rebaptized, it may be difficult, if not impossible, to dissuade them. But they come to this impasse because they have not been taught the deepest meanings of the sacrament. Often they are simply repeating superficial understandings that have been passed along to them. Solid sacramental teaching on a long-term basis is overdue, and only its serious pursuit will alleviate the frequent requests for rebaptism that characterize the church today.

## WHO CONSTITUTE SPECIAL CASES?

As every pastor knows well, cases arise that are not neatly covered by the assertion that baptism is for the committed and their children who are unbaptized. It is not wise to extend the statement of eligibility to include unusual and difficult cases. Still, we need to look at such situations from a pastoral perspective in an effort to understand how best to deal with them.

A common special case is that of emergency baptism. A distraught father phones the pastor from the hospital. "My wife just had a baby," he says. "The doctor tells us the baby probably will not live more than a few hours. Can you come over and baptize our child?" The theologically astute pastor can think of several reasons to decline the request. Baptism is not a magical action which will heal a dying infant, nor is it something which must be administered to prevent the eternal damnation of the infant after death. The rite ought to be administered in a liturgical setting, not in a hospital nursery where it may not even be possible to gather two or three church members as a kind of representative congregation. And perhaps the parents making the requests are not committed Christians.

Or possibly the request will come further along in the life cycle: "My husband," says the caller, "was critically injured in an accident and is asking to be baptized. Will you come?" In the mind of the pastor there arise responses similar to that in the instance of the dying infant.

Yet in both situations, the pastor usually honors the request. Is this action justified in light of the meaning of baptism we have set forth, or is the decision to administer the sacrament simply evidence of lack of pastoral backbone, or of acquiescence based on sentiment rather than on sound theology? The answer lies in the recognition that there is such a thing as pastoral theology that draws upon systematic theology and yet knows that the textbooks on doctrine cannot cover all cases, and that the gospel is offered to those in deep human need. It is not out of line to recall that Jesus healed on the sabbath and allowed his hungry disciples to pluck grain on that day, despite clear prohibitions against these actions, and despite the fact that probably he himself could have mustered convincing arguments as to why such healing and harvesting were improper.

The pastoral reality is that the parents and the dying man need tangible assurance of the graciousness of God and of incorporation into a supporting community. Granted, those who make such requests may also harbor misguided notions about the automatic damnation of the unbaptized; or they may secretly hope that the sacrament will bring a healing miracle to those who receive it. In part, their reasons for requesting the rite may even be irrational. How the parents or the accident victim will respond to their part of the covenant if death does not occur may be exceedingly unclear. But in the present instances, neither reasoned systems of dogmatics nor exhortations on covenant responsibility will accomplish much. Pastoral instinct says, "Go. Baptize. Explain and exhort later, if necessary."

This final statement is crucial, however. For the failure to heed it has unnecessarily increased the very requests and misunderstandings we are discussing. If the baptized person dies, at some opportune point in the grief process the pastor should help the family work through the fact that the rite is not a protection against death; rather, through baptism, the love of God and the care of the church for the deceased and for the family are proclaimed. The sacrament says something not only about and to the dying person, but also about and to the survivors: those who trust that the deceased is under the mercy and in the care of God now should gladly respond in grateful commitment within the community of faith. Unless this is communicated to the family of the person who has died after baptism, the administration of the rite to the dying will only reinforce misconceptions, and generate more requests of the same kind.

But suppose the person who is baptized regains health. Then the implications of the baptismal covenant need to be worked through. Therefore, those baptized should be presented to the congregation during a service of worship, with the congregation engaging in appropriate acts of welcome and mutual commitment. In many instances, a public reaffirmation of the baptismal covenant is appropriate. In all cases, steps should be taken to graft the newly baptized person into the life of the parish.

The retarded and the senile present another special case as baptismal candidates. Persons who are less than fully competent mentally have often been ignored by the church, much to our shame. Churches that baptize infants have administered the sacrament to infants whose retardation was not yet evident, only to cast off responsibility for continued nurture once the deficiency became apparent. In churches which baptize only at a later age, the retarded have sometimes been quietly passed over when others of their age were initiated. And what of the senile adult who repeatedly requests baptism, but is dismissed as being "too confused to know what she is saying," let alone to articulate the faith and live it out day by day? While we may never refer to the mentally retarded or senile as "sub-Christian," their marginal status in the congregation often gives the impression that this is how we feel. Sometimes it is patronizingly said that such persons are exempt from the usual requirement of faith, or that they possess some special kind of faith unlike that of other believers; therefore baptism is not considered helpful in their cases.

Two factors need to be considered here. First, the baptism of retarded or senile persons may be not only helpful, but actually necessary, for the sake of the congregation as a whole. Its administration forces "normal" people to confront the fact that divine love is intended for all, not just for those who reach a certain level of intellectual capacity. Furthermore, the presence of the less than fully competent within the congregation can be a means of judgment and grace for other members of the parish. Those who can grasp little of the nuances of doctrine may yet attend regularly and stay after services to put hymnals back in pew racks, or remain after meetings to straighten up chairs, while others dash out to play golf or chatter. A person struck dumb by a brain injury may bow the head and fold the hands in prayer, while other worshipers fidget and allow their minds to wander during the liturgy. Pastors frequently report levels of spiritual awareness among the retarded or senile which surpass our expectations of them. Their presence among us can be truly edifying.

But there is another and more important consideration. Behind the sacramental neglect of those who are not fully competent lies a failure to understand one thing that distinguishes the sacraments from the more exclusively verbal and reasoned expressions of the gospel. While the sacraments employ words, they operate primarily at the level of action that can be perceived visually, kinesthetically, and through the experiences of touch, non-verbal sound (as the water is laved or the wine poured, as well as in music) and taste and smell (in acts that may accompany the use of water in baptism, and in the Eucharist). Is it outrageous to suppose that God has chosen these very means in order to communicate in a special way with those who cannot comprehend sermons or grasp what is going on in a study session?

It is well known, for example, that the retarded often are more visibly affectionate than many of the rest of us. May it be that God offers to them a particular communication of the gospel in the laying on of hands and the kiss of peace after the administration of the water in baptism? If we withhold the sacrament from them because "they do not understand what it is all about," we may be robbing them of the very means of grace God has adapted to their special needs; and in the process we reveal the fact that actually it is we who do not understand what the sacrament is all about. Reconsideration of the baptism of the retarded and the senile is imperative. An honest appraisal of our assumptions may well result in the reversal of past policies and practices.

A third special case related to baptism springs from a conviction held by some persons that baptism is to be administered "in the name of Jesus only." This notion is based primarily upon certain passages in the Book of the Acts in which no Trinitarian formula or allusion is reported in connection with baptism. Two difficult situations present themselves in light of this belief. First, can we honor the request of those who come requesting baptism in the name of Jesus only? Second, can we transfer into our congregations those who previously were baptized in the name of Jesus only, or is that previous baptism to be considered illegitimate? The two cases must be resolved rather differently.

The request for baptism in the name of Jesus only is as simplistic and parochial as it is sincere. It fails to come to terms with the growth in the understanding of baptism within the New Testament itself. It is now acknowledged in most quarters that Christology developed over a period of years, and that the traces of its various stages of development are found within the New Testament. As the doctrine of Christ matured, so necessarily did the church's understanding of the meaning of his baptism and of our baptism into him. While only intimations can be given here concerning the historical development of the understanding of baptism in relation to an evolving Christology, the attempt to sketch the process in broad strokes is necessary if the difficulty in the "Jesus only" position is to be recognized.

In Paul's writing, and particularly in his use of earlier sources, Jesus' messiahship is bound up with his death and resurrection. (In particular, see Philippians 2:5-11, which Paul likely borrowed and emended at verse 9; and Romans 1:4, which may have been a formula already known at Rome rather than an original Pauline statement.) If Paul knew anything about Jesus' baptism by John, he gives no hint of it; but he emphatically connects our baptism into Christ with the Lord's death and resurrection—the focus of his messiahship (e.g., Rom. 6:3-11).

Mark, writing later, reports the baptism of Jesus and regards it as the moment of the announcement (perhaps even of the election) of Jesus as God's beloved Son. For Mark, as for Paul, the essence of messiahship is suffering, death, and resurrection. The baptism in the Jordan is an anticipation of the baptism on the cross; our baptism is seen as an initiation into suffering servanthood (Mark 10:35-45).

For Matthew, who wrote still later, messiahship was proclaimed publicly at Jesus' baptism. (In Mark, the voice from heaven seems to be addressed to Jesus; but in Matthew it is addressed to the crowd.) Nevertheless, the nature of Jesus had been revealed to select persons from the moment of Jesus' conception and birth, according to Matthew. At the end of the first Gospel, the risen and exalted Lord gives the church a command to proclaim his dominion to all, and in this connection, to baptize. Thus for Matthew the revelation has an expanding thrust. What is made known to only a few at the beginning and then remains hidden for thirty years is more widely proclaimed at the Jordan, though still only to a select group of Jews; but after the passion, death, and resurrection, the truth is mandated for universal proclamation. Thus, Christ's disciples are more than suffering servants; they are missionary emissaries of the Risen One who has begun his eschatological reign over the whole creation.

In the Johannine literature of a still later time, the Logos, which becomes incarnate, is already active in creation. As the Johannine Christology is more cosmic than that of the earlier writers, so also is John's view of the Lord's baptism and its implications for us. The One baptized in the Jordan is the Lamb of God (John 1:29) whose book of life has existed from the foundation of the world (Rev. 13:8). His death is not a disaster, even momentarily (as it seems to be in Mark and Matthew), but is a divine victory, a fulfillment of eternal design. Christ is entirely in control of his destiny (John 10:17-18), and his final word from the cross means, "I have finished my intended work of redemption. The long-pursued goal is reached." This victory is mediated sacramentally; for blood and water flow from his pierced side, alluding to the Eucharist and baptism. Thus baptism is not merely into the church on earth, but into the eternal work of redemption. The baptized are born from above by the Spirit (John 3:5-8) in perpetuation of the activity of the Risen Lord who constituted his church by breathing the Spirit upon the disciples (John 20:22).

It is clear that there is a development of the understanding of baptism that continues over a long period of time and that has left its traces in the New Testament documents. It is unfortunate that this development is so threatening to some Christians in our day. An evolving theology does not imply disharmony and rejection of earlier levels of understanding. Rather, each new insight builds upon and complements what has preceded it. We who are at the end of the process stand to gain much from it. Therefore, to advocate fixation at some early stage, as in the case of the "Jesus only" view, is tragic. Luke, in writing Acts, was not prescribing a rigid formula for posterity but, we may assume, was being relatively faithful as a chronicler in reporting a practice of the church in its earliest years. The church can no more give up the fully developed New Testament understanding of baptism than it can renounce the Christology of the mature New Testament period and, even later, of the Councils of Chalcedon and Nicaea. As Christians, we must take historical development seriously and appreciate its benefits, for God is a God of history. This the "Jesus only" position fails to recognize adequately.

The request for baptism in the name of Jesus only is also destructively parochial. It ignores the ecumenical reality of the church in favor of the preferences of a few who claim special insight. It is of no small importance that the whole church has been in accord regarding the Trinitarian baptismal formula for many centuries. Because baptism is our incorporation into the church catholic, to set aside that common formula comes close to being a self-contradiction. It tends toward the notion we have already rejected that we are baptized into a denomination or sect.

For these reasons, requests for baptism in the name of Jesus only cannot be honored, no matter how pious those making the request may be. Pastoral concern and patience are needed in working with such people in order to bring them to a fuller understanding of what baptism is.

Now consider a situation that is related, yet different. Someone comes to the pastor saying, "I was baptized several years ago in the name of Jesus only. Now I realize the limitations of that view and want to become a member of a congregation and denomination that uses the Trinitarian form. Do I need to be baptized in the Name of Trinity?" On the basis of what has been said in previous paragraphs, it seems that the logical answer is, yes. But here we must take into consideration our earlier discussion about the impossibility of rebaptism.

In addition to the usual considerations about rebaptism, in this instance performing the rite again would call into question even more than usual the integrity of the community of faith in which the original baptism took place. Christian love and respect impel us to refrain from implying that such groups are not Christian, no matter how simplistic and parochial their outlook may be. Precedents, both ancient and modern, are helpful; recall the fourth-century decision not to administer baptism to those coming from schismatic groups provided such persons verbally acknowledged the catholic faith. Note also may be taken that, in our day, some of those who baptize only in a certain manner or after a certain age nevertheless recognize baptism done by other modes or at earlier ages.

The answer to the whole problem of the "Jesus only"

preference is complex and may seem contradictory: we cannot administer baptism in the name of Jesus only, yet we accept it when those so initiated by other groups meet our doctrinal and other standards for membership. Clumsy as this approach may sound, any other policy presents even more difficulties.

A fourth special case is constituted by members of the Society of Friends (Quakers), the Salvation Army, and a few other groups that do not employ sacramental rites. Often they insist that they do observe baptism and the Lord's Supper according to Christ's command, but that they do this as he intended it to be done—spiritually, without dependence upon ritual actions and physical elements. Thus such groups are known technically as "spiritual baptists." To a certain extent, in the overall economy of the catholic church, these Christians serve to remind the rest of us of the dangers of sacramental practice when it becomes an idolatrous dependence or a meaningless habit whose motions we go through for the sake of tradition only. Still, we cannot view the position of the spiritual baptists as normative.

What then if a member of one of these groups wishes to join a congregation of a sacramental church but insists that spiritual baptism should be accepted as complete without the administration of water? Several approaches are possible. Probably the most common tactic is to exhort such persons to obey Christ's command in Matthew 28:19. Usually this avails little, however. The spiritual baptist is likely to respond that the command has already been obeyed, or will comply grudgingly rather than in the joyful manner that ought to characterize Christian obedience.

A more positive approach to the spiritual baptist is to probe underlying assumptions and motivations. Does the candidate for membership wish to receive the Lord's Supper regularly with the congregation? If so, why is one sacrament rejected while the other is desired? If not, why is membership sought in a family whose basic traditions are alien? It is well to seek to determine whether rejection of the sacraments springs merely from a desire to warn against possible abuses of sacramental practice, or from a deep-seated suspicion that God is opposed to the material world and that a choice between the two must be made. If such a suspicion exists, then what does the spiritual baptist make of the doctrines of creation and Incarnation?

Only through such careful exploration can we help to alleviate misconceptions about the nature of the sacraments. If the spiritual baptists continue to object to sacramental practice, it may be best to recommend that they retain membership in the group that supports their belief. Where a worshiping congregation of that group is not conveniently located to allow for active participation, certainly the non-sacramental activities of our churches are still open to such people.

A final category for consideration of special cases pertains to requests for "infant dedication." Within almost every denomination that baptizes infants there are parents who prefer to defer the sacrament until the children can decide for themselves in favor of (or against) its administration. Frequently such parents desire liturgical recognition in lieu of baptism; for this purpose there has arisen informally a "service of infant dedication."

Those who believe that the baptism of infants was not a biblical practice, and therefore is not to be observed, need to face the fact that neither was the dedication of infants a biblical rite. It is a quite recent innovation. Appeals to Hannah's giving of Samuel to the Lord or to the presentation of Jesus in the temple as precedents are misreadings of Scripture. In I Samuel 1:28 as translated in Today's English Version, Hannah is said to have *dedicated* her son, but the word used in the Hebrew text does not support this translation. The Revised Standard Version follows the King James Version in saying that Hannah "lent" Samuel to the Lord; the Jerusalem Bible is probably the most accurate in rendering the Hebrew as, "Now I make him over to Yahweh for the rest of his life."

The presentation of Jesus in the temple was related to the Hebrew custom of redeeming (buying back) the first male child, who was considered to belong to God at birth (Num. 18:15-16). This may reflect the Hebrews' rejection of the sacrifice of the first-born found in other cultures. In any event, the action of Mary and Joseph was quite unlike that of Hannah. In a very irregular act, Hannah gave her son to the Lord in a practical sense by leaving him in the keeping of Eli at Shiloh. In a quite customary act, Jesus was bought back from the Lord in a cultic sense. The Today's English Version also uses *dedicate* in Luke 2:23 (a citation of Exod. 13:12-13); but this translation is imprecise and out of step with versions that seek to follow the original text strictly, rather than to render it freely into basic English.

*Dedication* (or *devotion* as it is alternately translated) in the strictest biblical sense has to do with relinquishing or even destroying things utterly to the glory of God (see Lev. 22:2, 27:28-29). The Greek word that corresponds to the Hebrew term is found only once in the New Testament—in reference to the Feast of the Dedication of the Temple in Jerusalem (John 10:22). Thus, there is no New Testament basis for a service of the dedication of infants.

A more acceptable alternative liturgical form centers upon thanksgiving for the birth or adoption of a child. Contemporary forms by the Consultation on Church Union and the Episcopal Church are available.[10] The primary uses of such liturgies in the sacramental churches exist when the baptism of a child is to be preceded by another rite, when the request for baptism cannot be granted for one reason or another and the thanksgiving rite is to be a substitute, or when a child previously baptized has been adopted and liturgical recognition of this action is desired. Use of a rite of thanksgiving in the sacramental churches, because certain parents object to the baptism of infants, must be regarded as an irregular practice and not be encouraged.

If such a thanksgiving rite is used, however, great care should be taken that it not be confused with baptism and that it not be given a status that seems to place it on par with the sacrament. It should not, for example, be conducted at the baptismal font. Furthermore, the wording of the thanksgiving rite should not closely resemble that of the baptismal liturgy, lest the two be confused. Finally, it is desirable that such a thanksgiving rite include statements that point forward to baptism, even when this anticipation of the sacrament will not be fulfilled for a number of years.

These, then, are the common categories of special cases pastors are likely to confront in relation to baptism. Each category presents its own complexities, but all of them need to be addressed with careful theological understanding and patient pastoral graciousness.

## WHO ARE THE PROPER MINISTERS OF BAPTISM?

The question of who may properly administer baptism can be answered in several ways.

In times when the church considered baptism to be necessary for the salvation of the individual, the answer to the question about proper ministers was very broad: anyone is a proper minister who intends to do what the church does. That is, an actor who performs a baptismal ceremony on stage or someone who is jesting is not truly a minister of baptism, even though the correct words are said and the necessary actions done properly, for such a person does not really *intend* to baptize. But in very extreme circumstances, even a person of another religion could be the proper minister of baptism if no Christian were available. Even today, nurses and members of rescue squads are sometimes given instructions about how to baptize in emergency situations. The theology under which we are working does not encourage such latitude, however. The dangers of abuse and misunderstanding about the meaning of the rite are far greater than are the possible benefits to be gained in such instances.

Another answer to the question about proper administrators is that, in principle, all baptized Christians may baptize. Early in the third century, Tertullian, a Christian leader in North Africa, stated this worthy assertion, which establishes that the ministry of baptism is not the exercise of some magical power, nor is it the prerogative of an elite group. All can share equally what they themselves have received equally. When it came to practice as distinct from principle, Tertullian was more restrained:

It remains to me to advise you of the rules to be observed in giving and receiving baptism. The supreme right of giving it belongs to the high priest, which is the bishop; after him, to the presbyters and deacons, yet not without commission from the bishop, on account of the Church's dignity: for when this is safe, peace is safe. Except for that, even laymen have the right: "for that which is received on equal terms can be given on equal terms . . . that is, as the word ought not to be hidden by any man, so likewise baptism, which is no less declared to be 'of God,' can be administered by all."[11]

In speaking of the importance of the church's dignity and peace, Tertullian probably had in mind the same kinds of matters that caused Paul to tell the Corinthians that, while they enjoyed a certain freedom in worship, yet "all things should be done decently and in order" (I Cor. 14:40). Someone must preside over the worshiping assembly if liturgical anarchy is to be avoided. This person needs to understand thoroughly the meaning and manner of liturgical action and needs to be able to represent the whole congregation and even the whole church catholic. God has provided for such needs through a called ministry; the church has confirmed this provision through election to ordination and the education of those ordained. Normally, therefore, those selected and trained preside over baptism, as over other liturgical functions. This delegation of liturgical leadership is in no way a denial of our equality before God through baptism, but is simply a recognition of the fact that those elected to the ordained ministry can represent all who elect them, and are charged with exercizing oversight with particular responsibility for teaching and church discipline.

Since the church selects particular people to act as representative ministers on behalf of the whole body, the church does not give the role of presiding over the baptismal liturgy to the laity, while the clergy who have been so selected look on passively. In churches that have bishops, these chief shepherds should take seriously their function as baptismal ministers, heeding the advice of Tertullian. This is not to say that baptism by a bishop is somehow superior, or confers special status upon the baptized. But bishops can be seen as visible reminders of the catholicity of the church; because they have jurisdiction over a number of parishes and have a collegial relationship with other bishops, in a unique way they remind the individual congregation that there is more to the church of Jesus Christ into which we are baptized than the people of one particular parish. Bishops may well administer baptism in the course of regular episcopal visitation, particularly when they are coming for the rite of confirmation, which best takes place within the baptismal liturgy.

In churches that have deacons, these clergy traditionally have had the authority to preside at baptism; normally, when a bishop is not present, an elder (presbyter, priest) will preside, however. When for good reason a member of the clergy who is not the pastor of the congregation has been invited to participate, it will nevertheless be the pastor who presides in the absence of the bishop, even though the visiting minister is given an important role in the service.

A visiting minister will accept an invitation to participate in a baptism only if the incumbent pastor extends the request. This is particularly important when the visitor is a former pastor of the congregation. Otherwise, clergy find themselves caught in a popularity contest that, in itself, obscures the representative function of the clergy. Even so, previous pastors properly invited may well indicate that they prefer to attend the rite as members of the congregation. Strict adherence to this ministerial etiquette will do much to preserve the church's dignity and peace by way of establishing the fact that the ministers of baptism represent the assembly over which they preside, and are not free agents of the sacrament.

Because baptism is incorporation into Christ's church, it is inescapably a corporate rite. Baptism without a congregation present is a bit like a wedding at which only one of the prospective marriage partners arrives. The phrase "private baptism" is a contradiction in terms, and the continuation of non-congregational rites should not be tolerated. Even in emergencies, it is highly desirable that the clergy be accompanied by one or more lay persons; indeed, some denominations rightly require this. While the ordained clergy are representative ministers, they are intended more to speak on behalf of the congregation that is present than to act in the stead of an absent congregation.

Within the congregational service, the assembly should assume a vow of responsibility for the nurture of the newly baptized (in the case of adults as well as of infants), and should extend a cordial welcome to those initiated into their company. We should, however, go beyond this rather minimal participation. The Scripture lessons may well be read by persons from the congregation who are prepared for this task. An officer of the congregation may introduce the candidates to the whole assembly as the baptismal rite begins. If water is to be carried in procession to fill the font, a member of the congregation may do this. Unless there are denominational restrictions against it, when the laying on of hands is observed, members of the congregation may join the clergy and members of the family of the person being baptized in carrying out this action. A lay person appropriately leads the intercessions for the newly baptized.

It is also important to explore ways of representing the church catholic in the baptismal service. The liturgical role of the clergy is one aspect of this wider vision; for while they represent the congregation in their presiding role, all clergy (not only bishops) also represent the larger church. But more than a clerical manifestation of catholicity is needed. One possibility is for congregations of various denominations to share in baptismal rites, where polity permits this. In the service of a local United Methodist congregation, for example, the lessons for the day might be read respectively by a Lutheran, a Roman Catholic, and a Presbyterian. These representatives from other parishes might also join in the laying on of hands, where this is allowed.

Another possibility is for several congregations to hold a joint baptismal service, using a liturgy acceptable to all. Such activities must have a clear congregational base, with reasonable expectation that each parish participating will be well represented. Baptisms should not take place at church conventions, for example, since each congregation sends only a limited number of delegates to such a gathering.

If such interaction between congregations is not possible, at least a congregation can take note of when baptisms are occurring in neighboring parishes, and on that day include in their prayers of intercession the newly baptized and the congregations into which they come. Such a practice can counteract parochialism and promote a sense of the ecumenical community, even where current policies prohibit joint participation in worship across denominational lines. Indeed, our remembrance of one another through prayer in this manner may be a most effective tool in bringing about the abolition of the prohibitions that deny the unity given to us in baptism.

The practice of having sponsors at baptism requires re-evaluation. In some congregations use of sponsors becomes an easy out; the delegation of this responsibility to a few prevents others from seeing the ministry the whole congregation has to the newly baptized. But other congregations use sponsors on the assumption that what is everybody's business usually turns out to be nobody's business. When sponsors are used, their role should be clearly defined. They are not figureheads, and their role is not honorific. They are active representatives of, but not substitutes for, the whole congregation. Regardless of the age of the person baptized, the sponsors have a responsibility, not merely before and during the rite, but afterward.

It is best for sponsors to be assigned to candidates, rather than being selected by the candidates or their parents. This lessens the danger of a popularity contest approach, and insures that the sponsors will come from within the congregation so that they can relate the newly baptized to the congregation. A carefully considered process of selecting, training, holding accountable, and evaluating the sponsors will broaden the base of congregational involvement so that the sponsors are seen as truly being representative of the whole.

In planning the baptismal service, care should be taken to include as participants in the liturgy those who reflect the diversity of the congregation in all possible ways: persons of various ages (including baptized children), of both sexes, of various ethnic backgrounds and races, and so on. In this way, we demonstrate the fullness of the community and ministry into which the newly baptized are called, and we emphasize the fact that all in the congregation share in the act of baptizing.

## IS BAPTISM NECESSARY FOR *WHOSE* SALVATION?

At this point someone is certain to be asking, "Why all this fuss about proper candidates, ministers, and procedures? After all, baptism isn't necessary for salvation, is it?" At one time, of course, almost everyone considered it to be so, and some still do.[12] Now many have come to doubt the efficacy of baptism, let alone its necessity. The earlier assertion that it is not necessary to baptize the dying out of fear of damnation should not be taken to mean that baptism has nothing to do with salvation. We need to look more deeply at the issue by changing our question from, "Is baptism necessary for salvation?" to, "Is baptism necessary for *whose* salvation?"

We can gain much insight by reflecting upon these words of Peter Taylor Forsyth, a British Congregationalist theologian early in this century:

> Sacraments are not primarily *individual* acts. They are corporate acts, acts *of the Church*. . . . Baptism is not primarily an act of the parent nor of the child, but of the Church and of Christ in the Church. It is our individualism that has done most to ruin the sacrament of Baptism among us. We get a wrong answer because we do not put the right question. We ask, What good does Baptism do for me or that child? instead of, What is the active witness and service the Church renders to the active Word of Christ's Gospel in the Baptism of young or old?

> Sacraments are necessary for the health of the Church. Baptism is necessary for the weal of the Church, whose act it chiefly is. Therefore it is necessary for the world the Church has to convert.[13]

Forsyth correctly pointed out that individualism has had a destructive effect upon our thinking. But so also has our penchant for defining salvation in legalistic ways. We want to know exactly who is saved and when the salvation took effect (or ceases to be effective). The problem has been made worse by discussions concerning whether or not baptism has been valid in certain cases, on the assumption that validity could be precisely defined and determined. Thus, baptism is seen, not as a dynamic activity of Christ through which the gospel comes to us, but as a mechanical action of the church by means of which salvation is transmitted to those being baptized. But salvation is not a commodity that comes off of a conveyor belt in a hermetically sealed container. Salvation is healing that results in life; it is characterized by an elusive energy. When its mystery is removed by attempts at overly precise definition, it is destroyed.

The Nicene Creed contains a magnificent affirmation that "we acknowledge one baptism for the forgiveness of sins." This has sometimes been misunderstood to mean that at the very moment of administration baptism cancels the sins of the person baptized and effects salvation for ever. But the two statements do not have the same meaning at all. Rightly understood, baptism has to do with the church as a whole, the church catholic. Baptism is not something that happens to us only once, to be forgotten or looked upon as a time of a change in our legal status before God. The rite of initiation brings us into covenant with God and into the community of the covenant where the promises and claims of God are set before us continually. Baptism sets into motion a dynamic of life that defies legal precision or even clear definition. The forgiveness of sins implies interrelationships, life in community with God and with one another. We do acknowledge one baptism for the forgiveness of sins, precisely because baptism prevents us from indulging in the isolation of self-idolatory and incorporates us into the community in which the Spirit works continually to win our allegiance to righteousness and to prepare us for our witness to the world.

Again we turn to the wisdom of P. T. Forsyth regarding baptism as a congregational act. Here Forsyth is speaking especially about the baptism of infants; but what he says is equally true in the case of the baptism of adults. His comments enable us to see who it is we are talking about when we ask, "Is baptism necessary for salvation?"

The Baptism of every infant should be a renewed Baptism for every adult present. Every baptized adult should feel it a Christian duty and happiness to be present. . . . And it should be an occasion when they go back to the meaning of their own Baptism, and ask themselves whether it was an empty form or the hand of Christ laid on them by the long, long arm of the Church to claim them for a regenerate destiny. They should examine themselves how far they have kept the faith for which they were claimed, and have cleaved to the Cross by which they were bought. They were claimed and set apart as Christ's in Baptism by Christ's Church in His behalf. Have they continued Christ's? . . . Baptism does not mainly concern the child or parents, I repeat. It is an act principally for the Church. The whole Church in faith and spirit enters the cleansing stream. It revives by faith its sense of the new and eternal life of forgiveness. It measures its own faithfulness to its regenerative redemption. It makes profession by Baptism of its faith in the New Creation. It utters its repentance. And it resolves anew, prays anew, to be faithful to the end, to keep and renew its Baptism till death.[14]

It is this theme of keeping and renewing baptism until death that we now take up.

# 4

# TO KEEP AND RENEW
# UNTIL DEATH

## THE NECESSITY AND NATURE OF RENEWAL

Unlike God, who is faithful to all covenant promises, we are fickle. Even when our intentions are the best, our actions do not match our desires. The covenant we make with God is therefore frequently broken by us and needs to be renewed by us. The call to renewal is often stressed in preaching, particularly through sermons on texts such as that in which Jesus speaks about taking up the cross daily in order to follow him.

Luther sought to emphasize the daily renewal of the baptismal covenant by suggesting to his followers that, each morning upon arising, they place a hand upon the head (where the water of the sacrament had been applied) and say, "I am baptized." But that practice has been neglected, and most Protestants have little awareness of the need for the regular renewal of the covenant, still less of the relation between this daily renewal and the initial act of baptism itself. There are, however, liturgical occasions that bring renewal to the center of attention.

The renewal of baptism has been explicit in much Protestant understanding of confirmation. The promise of God is confirmed to believers, we have been told, (particularly to those who were baptized in infancy); the believers, in turn, confirm their covenant with God by giving public testimony to their faith. In the Anglican liturgical tradition, for example, the confirmation rite begins with a question concerning whether those who come to be confirmed do renew the solemn promise and vow made at their baptism.

Two problems are inherent in confirmation as a form of baptismal renewal, however. First, as we shall see in detail in later chapters, confirmation as covenant renewal is a far cry from the meaning attached to the laying on of hands and associated rites in the early centuries of the church. Only when this imposition of hands became detached from baptism itself by an extended period of time could confirmation take on the character of an act of renewal. Second, confirmation as generally practiced is unrepeatable; thus, it does not adequately reflect the need for continual renewal.

To do justice to the dynamics of the baptismal covenant set forth in the first three chapters, we need a form of renewal that is corporate (not individualistic, as confirmation tends to be), clearly related to the sacrament of baptism, and repeatable. Such forms are provided in recent liturgical revisions by major denominations. Since the restoration of the Easter Vigil in 1951, baptismal renewal by the congregation at the celebration of the Lord's death and resurrection has become increasingly important in the Roman Catholic Church. Contemporary liturgical formulations for Episcopalians, Lutherans, and United Methodists all stress that confirmation is a form of baptismal renewal in which the congregation, as well as the confirmands, join; these same denominations also associate corporate renewal with the Paschal Vigil or other Easter rites. Episcopalians and Lutherans include a public act of renewal for those who transfer to their denominations from other denominations, and for those who have become inactive members and wish to be restored to active membership. In addition to these occasions, United Methodists suggest public acts of renewal for those transferring from one congregation to another within the denomination, and for individuals who wish to testify to some important spiritual experience in their lives, even if this does not follow a lapse of active membership.

The actual forms of renewal vary from one denomination to another. Episcopalians and Lutherans do not use the laying on of hands except at confirmation; for United Methodists, however, the laying on of hands is a repeatable act that occurs at baptism, at confirmation, and at any subsequent acts of public renewal by individuals (though hands are not placed upon the entire congregation in rites of corporate renewal). United Methodists suggest that on any occasion of baptismal renewal (including congregational) a small quantity of water be sprinkled toward those making their renewal as a reminder of baptism, although this is left to pastoral discretion. Lutherans suggest such sprinkling only at the Easter Vigil; Episcopalians do not mention it at all.

What is striking, however, is not the difference in detail from one rite to another, but the fact that all of these denominations have moved from associating liturgical renewal of baptism with confirmation alone (if at all) to a repeated liturgical renewal, in order to reflect the daily renewal of the covenant baptism implies. Furthermore, it is not unlikely that when United Church of Christ and Presbyterian liturgies are next revised, they will include a repeated act of baptismal renewal; for the concept of renewal is by no means alien to the Calvinistic tradition, even though liturgical expression is missing there, as it has been elsewhere until recently.

There is a difficulty in the fact that recently revised rites tend to run ahead of congregational understanding of the need for liturgical expressions of renewal. Congregations may be helped in this regard by looking at analogies in daily life. Our daily actions of breathing and eating are implicit renewals of our birth. Yet once a year most of us observe explicitly the occasion of birth with a certain amount of festivity. No matter how much we may complain about getting older, these birthday parties are expressions of our gratitude for life and reminders of the blessings and opportunities we may take for granted in the routine daily activities of breathing and eating. Thus, at a birthday celebration we employ particular ritual activities to highlight what may otherwise be overlooked. Candles are blown out to give evidence that the breath of life is very much in us; cake and ice cream are eaten year after year. The singing of the same birthday ditty is a mandatory ritual, and gifts are given as a matter of course, and in anticipation that life will continue for the foreseeable future. A birthday observance is an affirmation of life, a ritual by means of which we express periodically the daily renewal of birth. So it is not so strange that the renewal of baptism should be marked by certain ritual activities not normally associated with our daily devotion and service to God, yet clearly reminiscent of baptism: the reaffirmation of vows and perhaps the laying on of hands and sprinkling with water.

Furthermore, certain of our natural birthdays have a special significance because they signal particular responsibility and awareness of maturity. Usually, at puberty a significant birthday is singled out—the sixteenth, or the one that makes a person eligible for a driver's license or other adult privileges such as voting. Similarly, the renewal of the baptismal covenant is appropriately focused clearly by a particular act of renewal (usually called confirmation) when those baptized during infancy or childhood reach the age of responsibility. This particular act of renewal serves to remind us of the continuing character of our covenant. If confirmation in some quarters has come to be regarded as graduation from the church school, even as the point at which teen-agers bow out of regular church participation, then its purpose has been totally misunderstood. The conscious renewal of the covenant at puberty is intended to mark the beginning of an awareness about, and commitment to, continual renewal, just as a particular birthday reminds the teen-ager of the continuing privileges and responsibilities of adulthood.

Finally, in our daily lives, occasions arise, quite apart from the annual observance of our birth, that call for recognition and celebration. For example, a person who has returned to health after major surgery, or one who has narrowly escaped death in an accident or in war, may call together friends in order to celebrate. Similar occasions of festivity surround various experiences which give us a heightened sense of vitality: a job promotion, the running of a marathon or the making of a hole-in-one, the successful launching of a business venture. In a similar way, special acts of baptismal renewal are appropriate for those who have nearly died spiritually but have now recovered, and for those who have had a heightened experience of the grace of God in their lives. In many cases, an act of covenant renewal will answer the longing such people seek to fill by asking for rebaptism. Often those making this request do not doubt the covenant promise of God, but perceive that some outward sign of their commitment to the covenant is desirable.

When such analogies from daily experience can be drawn, people who at first may resist liturgical innovation can be helped to see that the recent rites of renewal are helpful, and even necessary. Occasional liturgical expression focuses our attention upon realities that otherwise we are likely to forget. What is strange is not that the church has recently introduced liturgical forms of renewal, but that for so long the church has neglected such forms.[1] Careful use of the rites of renewal remind us that our life in Christ is a continuous experience and that our commitment is to be renewed daily until death.

## BAPTISM AND THE EUCHARIST

Liturgical forms of baptismal renewal have never entirely disappeared from the life of the church, although, with the possible exception of confirmation, these forms have been implicit rather than explicit. The most important implicit form of renewal is the Lord's Supper, or Eucharist. As daily meals imply a desire to renew the life which begins with physical birth, so participation in this holy meal of the church implies a desire to renew our life in Christ. We need, therefore, to examine carefully the relationship between these two sacraments.

Throughout history, the church has insisted that the Eucharist is for the baptized, and thus is quite different from a church supper or coffee hour to which the general public may be invited. The intention is not to discriminate against or embarrass individuals who may be sincere but unbaptized; the purpose of the restriction is to indicate that the Lord's Supper is indeed a "holy" communion—distinctive, set apart from other forms of eating and drinking. The Supper is to be seen as more than a social gathering; those who come to the Lord's Table should recognize him in the breaking of bread, find in him the true source of life, and be joined in unity with him and one another. Baptism signifies precisely the enlightenment, the gift of divine life, and the incorporation into the community of faith that makes true eucharistic joy possible.

When we keep in mind the intention behind the restricting of the Table to the baptized, we are better able to deal with awkward situations. For example, it does not behoove pastors to pause at the communion rail to interrogate visitors on the chance that some of the prospective communicants may be unbaptized. Nor at a nuptial Eucharist will the server pass by those who come for communion but belong to the Society of Friends or the Salvation Army. When unbaptized worshipers regularly present themselves for communion, however, careful counsel is indicated. Such persons should be helped to think through their desire to receive the sacramental signs of spiritual nutrition and growth but not the sacramental sign of spiritual birth; or, as often seems to be the case, such persons need to face the fact that they see in baptism a commitment they are unwilling to make, but fail to see that this same commitment is implied in the Eucharist.

Indeed, there is a sense in which the Eucharist calls for commitment even more explicit than does baptism. The material gift of baptism is ours for the taking in the natural world. We do not produce water by the labor of our hands. Bread and wine, on the other hand, do presuppose human involvement. The grain and the grapes must be planted, tended, and harvested; then the bread and the wine must be made. Baptism and the Eucharist are thus complementary signs; the former reveals most clearly God's initiative, the latter our responsible participation in transforming what God provides in the natural order.

The Lord's Table is for those whom the Lord has claimed and incorporated into his body through baptism, for those to whom he has given an identity and responsibility as people of the new covenant in the new age. But is the Eucharist for all of the baptized, or only for some of them? The logical answer is "For all. Those to whom the Lord grants spiritual birth from above, the Lord also grants nourishment." Yet again and again the church has backed away from the obvious answer. Therefore, it is necessary to examine three major barriers that exist between the baptized and the Table of their Lord.

The oldest barrier, but the one least used today, is that of excommunication due to serious sin. Traditionally, notorious transgressors were barred from the Eucharist pending public repentance and restoration. Never was their baptism called into question; but like naughty children, they were sent to their rooms without dinner. Whether this form of church discipline was justified in times past is beside the point here. Suffice it to say that while the contemporary church is in great need of self-discipline, literal excommunication is likely to accomplish little in our age. Unfortunately, many who spurn the teaching of the church have so low a view of the Eucharist that barring them from it is like telling children that they are forbidden to eat a vegetable they don't like anyhow.

Our problem is to convince Christians that much of what passes for spiritual nutrition is, in fact, junk food, and that the Lord's Supper is the staple diet of the faithful. While it may be argued that the best way to stress the importance of the Eucharist is to make it inaccessible to all except the most committed, that is not a very good strategy; for admitting to communion only those who qualify under some form of discipline easily backfires. Not only does it keep away the uncommitted, but it may cause the overly conscientious to stay away because they fear they cannot measure up. If either baptism or the Lord's Supper is to function as a form of church discipline, baptism is the logical choice. Once admitted into the family, all members should be welcome at the family board.

A second barrier between the baptized and the Lord's Table is all too evident today; and while nearly everyone wants to see it removed, positive action is slow and painful. This barrier is exclusion on the basis of denominational affiliation. In certain denominations the feast of the Lord is open only to members of that denomination or members of certain designated denominations that share agreement in doctrine or practice at specified points. Those who so restrict communion feel they do so properly on the basis of church order. But since they generally recognize as valid the baptism of those whom they exclude, the excluded can justifiably ask: "How can you recognize that Christ has made me a part of his holy Church through baptism and yet fail to welcome me at his Table?" Despite the sincere reasons behind the exclusion, the failure to welcome faithful communicants from other denominations is a form of excommunication that causes deep pain to those excluded, and hinders the witness the church ought to present to the world of our unity in Christ.

There are two schools of thought concerning the way this problem may be overcome. One sees eucharistic fellowship as a source of unity: those who eat together will discover their true unity around the Lord's Table. Furthermore, restrictive rules tend to lag behind practice and are changed only after they are beyond reasonable possibility of enforcement. Therefore, it is suggested, prohibitions against inter-communion are to be ignored. Practice that which is technically illegal, says this school of thought; thus you will discover your real unity, and eventually the rules will be changed to conform to what actually has been taking place for some time. The other school of thought insists that table fellowship can only follow formal unity; indeed, to keep rules that appear foolish and inflict pain will goad us toward formal unity. Reinhold Niebuhr somewhere referred to this approach as "sacramental agony"—to worship with a company of persons who have been made your brothers and sisters in Christ through baptism, and yet to be unable to go with them to the Lord's Table, is to experience a deep spiritual pain that is capable of motivating reform.

Whether it will be most effective to follow the first course of action, the second, or some combination of the two, is not clear. But it is apparent that those who claim one Lord, one faith, and one baptism cannot be content until the one body of Christ is nourished about the same table. A proper understanding of baptism makes the permanent acceptance of exclusion on the basis of denominational membership intolerable.

A third major barrier to the communion of all baptized persons is based upon judgments regarding physical and mental development. In the recent past, both Roman Catholics and Protestants have assumed that baptized persons are not to receive communion until they reach a certain stage of development. It has often been taken for granted that retarded and senile persons also are barred from communion, or at least discouraged from receiving it, either because they cannot attain the proper level of cognitive ability or have slipped from it. This barrier between the baptized and the Lord's Table rests upon a subtle and questionable assumption: that we must understand the Eucharist rationally and be capable of articulating that understanding before we may receive the sacrament. This assumption needs to be challenged by important historic witness and pastoral experiences.

To begin with, the proscription against giving infants communion is not of great duration and has not been universal. In the Eastern Orthodox bodies, infants are given communion from the moment of baptism onward; for centuries in the West the same practice was observed but disappeared, as we will see in chapter 6, for reasons related to historical circumstance rather than to theology. Among Protestants, Methodists in particular have stood as an exception to the exclusion of young children from the Lord's Table; it is not uncommon to see family members of all ages receiving the elements together in Methodist churches.[2]

Further, we are confronted by a practice in the ancient church that seems strange to us if we view communion as a matter of cognitive understanding. In the early centuries, adults who were converting to the faith received baptism and the Eucharist in a single liturgical occasion, but were told very little about either sacrament in advance. This was hardly due to lack of time, for the candidates went through a period of instruction prior to baptism lasting up to three years. After they received the rites of initiation, the new Christians came to church daily and were told the meaning of the sacraments. Apparently it was assumed that the sacraments are divine mysteries even adults cannot begin to understand until they have participated in them; the sacraments are experiences before they are doctrines or explanations. (This assumption is emphasized by the fact that at least as early as the time of Hippolytus in the late second or early third century, children were baptized and given communion; though they could not explain these events, children could experience them, and it was taken for granted that they should.)

Pastoral experience today challenges the exclusion of persons on the basis of mental capacity. Many pastors report that children in the congregation seem to be readily benefited by receiving communion, for they know very early in life what it means to be included or excluded when food is served. This is no trivial matter because baptism signifies our inclusion in the family of God. Recently I was invited to help administer the Eucharist on the Day of Pentecost by a pastor whose congregation included several dozen students from a school for the mentally handicapped. On that occasion, many adult communicants, presumably well informed as to the meaning of the sacrament, came forward with staid manners and somber countenance. The retarded children, however, approached with faces wreathed in smiles and hands outstretched to receive with joy the gifts of the Lord. They, it seemed to me, comprehended what many of their "more competent" elders did not; and I cannot shake the conviction that the Holy Spirit spoke to those children in uniquely sacramental tongues so that they truly heard, each in his or her own language.

An equally strong case can be made for the communion of the senile on the basis of pastoral experience. A former student shared with me an incident that occurred when she was an associate pastor and her senior pastor had asked her to take communion to a faithful elderly parishioner in a nursing home. At the desk, the pastor was told: "Well, you may go in to visit her; but it will be useless to try to give her communion. She has not understood anything in months. She never says a sensible word, and does not even recognize her own children." Dutifully the associate pastor carried out the request of her superior, inwardly questioning, throughout, the wisdom of such action. The patient stared distractedly out of the window as the prayers were offered. She received the bread and wine with no apparent comprehension; but having done so, suddenly she looked at the pastor and said to her, "You know, God really does love us, doesn't he?" When I have told this story at clergy meetings, numerous pastors have come forward to share similar experiences that challenge the assumption that God speaks only to those whom the rest of us judge mentally competent.

Experiences of divine communication with the mentally handicapped through the sacraments help clarify the relationship between the sacraments and other forms of communicating the gospel. We may properly assume that a certain level of intellectual development is required for the hearing of a sermon or of a lecture on doctrine. But the sacraments are complementary to, not identical with, these more conceptual activities. The gospel is intended not only for those who possess mental abilities of a certain sort, but for all persons. It is not unreasonable to assume that through the sacraments God communicates in a very special way with those within the Christian community who are incapable of understanding more intellectual modes of address.

Before he was exiled from the Soviet Union, Aleksandr

Solzhenitsyn sent an eloquent plea to the Patriarch of Moscow for the freedom of the church; it included an entreaty that children not be discouraged from participation in the liturgy, despite pressure from the state on that point. Solzhenitsyn did not argue, as we might, that early learning is a helpful foundation upon which to build a mature faith later. Of more fundamental importance, he asserted that children are capable of perceiving a dimension of the liturgy that they may be unable to grasp later on. He said:

[I] saw before me my early childhood, spent in attending many church services, and remembered that initial impression, exceptionally fresh and pure, which later could not be erased by any millstone or mental theory. . . . After the baptizing of infants [in Russia] all of the child's associations with the church usually cease [when the church submits to government pressure to exclude children from the liturgy]. The doors to a religious upbringing are tightly shut against them. They are barred from participating in church services, taking communion, and perhaps, even from attending church. We are robbing our children by depriving them of that unrepeatable, purely angelic perception of the church service which in adult life can never be recaptured nor even understood as to what has been lost.[5]

Solzhenitsyn seems to suggest that the attainment of the age of reason (as we like to call it), far from being the appropriate time for admission to the Lord's Supper and other sacramental experiences, may actually put obstacles in the way of our spiritual perception. If this sounds like anti-intellectualism, we need only recall the disastrous effect Enlightenment thinking had upon sacramental practice in recent centuries. While the full story cannot be rehearsed here, a few incidents may be cited.

In the eighteenth century, English intellectuals (including Joseph Priestley, the discoverer of oxygen) revised the *Book of Common Prayer* by removing what could not be demonstrated by science, including sacramental emphasis, to say nothing of doctrinal affirmations about the Trinity, the divinity of Jesus Christ, and eschatology. Following the revolution of 1789, the cathedral of Notre Dame de Paris, among many others, was desecrated; the cross was torn from the altar, and the Goddess of Reason was enthroned in its place. In 1800, six communicants came to St. Paul's Cathedral in London on Easter Day—the one day on which the reception of communion was presumably obligatory. The sterility of the Enlightenment reforms is attested to by the facts that the Prayer Book stands today theologically unscathed (even in drastic contemporary revisions), that the cross is back upon the altar of Notre Dame, and that St. Paul's can expect a respectable gathering of communicants on Easter Day, at least.

This is not to say that reason is diametrically opposed to spiritual understanding, but rather that reason by itself is insufficient; it needs to be preceded and accompanied by other modes of perception and evaluation. God, who has created us whole persons, addresses us in the totality of our existence. When we filter out a part of the divine approach toward us, we hinder the work of God. That is why exclusion of the baptized from the Lord's Table is such a serious matter; whether it is based on discipline or denominationalism or rationalism, such exclusion deserves to be challenged.

## BAPTISM, CHURCH MEMBERSHIP, AND DISCIPLESHIP

Having surveyed the relationship between baptism, renewal, and the reception of the Eucharist, we turn now to two related matters. When do we become church members? Who is a Christian?

The answer to the first question has two aspects, one theological, the other administrative. Often there is a conflict between them. The theological answer is straightforward: we become members of Christ's church at baptism. But some denominations, whether simply by custom or through legislation, refer to an act of conscious commitment at puberty or later as the time when one "joins the church," even though baptism was received much earlier. This clearly implies that baptized persons are not necessarily members of the church.

Sensing the confusion such an approach entails, other denominations seek to clarify matters through the use of categories such as baptized but unconfirmed members, on the one hand, and confirmed members, on the other. This seems to imply that church membership is a process involving two distinct steps and reinforces the unfortunate notion that baptism in itself is incomplete. Other churches use categories such as preparatory members and full members: in addition to implying that baptism is not a full sacrament, such designations raise the perplexing issue we have discussed concerning assumptions about maturity as the basis for full acceptance by the church.

On the human level, do we regard our sons and daughters merely as preparatory members of our families until they reach a certain age? Do we not rather consider them full members of the family from birth, even though we rightly expect different things of them at each stage of development? In our natural families, fullness is based upon the potential that exists at the moment, not upon a level of attainment the person may be expected to achieve ten or fifteen years hence. In no sense do our children have to earn their places as family members; they are members because we have borne them and love them. In the best of circumstances, that love is unconditional, even though parents properly have expectations of their children. So, too, God seeks and desires our commitment and growth. But it is God's unconditional love that makes us members of Christ's church. In baptism God does not act half-way.

That churches need administrative categories of membership cannot be denied. But these should not be in conflict with the theological truth concerning baptism. If for legal purposes we need to differentiate between those who may vote in church meetings and those who may not, then the categories are best called "voting members" and "non-voting members." While admission into the voting category may involve attainment of a certain age based on ecclesiastical or civil statute, this does not eliminate the possibility that some baptized members beyond that age may be ineligible to vote by virtue of inactivity. This fact presents another possible administrative division: that of active and inactive members. Here the setting of standards, and the procedures of judging their attainment, is tricky. Sometimes frequency of attendance and reception of the Eucharist, together with the record of financial support, is used to judge activity; however, these do not necessarily reflect with accuracy a deep commitment to Christian ministry in the world.

While determining what constitutes active membership is by no means easy, the use of the categories "active" and "inactive" has two advantages. First, age is not the primary focus. Children may so live out their commitment to Christ in a commendable way as to be judged active; nor does reaching chronological adulthood guarantee an affirmative judgment. Second, all baptized persons are called members. Thus we point to God's action and expectation; God does not give up on us when we break our part of the covenant, but rather seeks our return to faithfulness. Those who have been unresponsive to the baptismal promises and then repent do not rejoin the church; they simply reaffirm or renew their part of the covenant. They act positively upon a membership that cannot be taken away from them.

Now we come to the second and thornier question: Who then are to be called Christians? Is every church member, no matter how uncommitted to the baptismal promises, a Christian? The question cannot be answered until we look at the variety of meanings the term *Christian* can carry with it.

One possible definition of *Christian* is the sociological one. A pollster appears at the door and asks, "Are you Christian, Jewish, Muslim, or the adherent of some other religion?" In most Western countries, anyone who is not intentionally a follower of Judaism or Islam will probably answer, "Christian." The response indicates nothing about the level of commitment, or even about baptism. Such an identification rests upon the assumption that "this is a Christian country" and therefore everyone who does not choose some other option is Christian by association (or default). To anyone serious about Christian discipleship, the weakness of the sociological definition is self-evident, and historically has been the source of much difficulty in the so-called Christian societies.

Another definition of the term *Christian* is related to doctrine. One is a Christian with reference to certain statements about the divinity and Lordship of Christ, about the Trinity, and so on. While this approach has had far more formal importance in the past than it has now, periodically it surfaces as the basis for break-away church movements or theological witch-hunts. Again, the weaknesses are evident: the possibility of intellectual rigidity, lack of charity, and the failure to accept human finitude when wrestling with truth, as well as the assumption that intellectual assent automatically leads to an active Christian witness in the world.

A third possible definition of *Christian* is ethical in orientation. Partially in response to the weaknesses of the first two definitions, Christians are sometimes identified on the basis of social values or style of life. One is deemed a Christian or a non-Christian because of views about abortion, nuclear disarmament, or the struggle for racial equality. Or, someone will say: "Oh, I do try to be a Christian. I don't work or shop on Sunday; I don't gamble or take the Lord's name in vain." (Or, depending upon the theological point of reference, "I don't dance, wear jewelry, or attend the movies.") While the social-consciousness standard and the personal morality standard may seem to be worlds apart, as in geometry, positions that are 180 degrees apart on a circle are nevertheless on the same plane. Both varieties of judgment appeal to the biblical assertion that "by their fruits you shall know them," but fail to take seriously the equally important biblical insight that fruits are the work of the Holy Spirit, not the means by which we earn salvation or attain spirituality. Further, it is dangerous (even potentially blasphemous) to define the term *Christian* on the basis of observable opinions or actions alone, particularly when the qualifications are determined solely by those who are doing the judging.

A fourth definition of *Christian* is the experiential one. Those persons are deemed Christians who have had (and can clearly articulate) a certain type of religious experience. Christians are those who "have been saved"—not with reference to the objective atoning work of Christ upon the cross nor even to personal commitment to discipleship in response to that objective work, but with respect to a specific emotional experience by means of which Christ's work is subjectively appropriated. Or, Christians are those who are "born again." Here the emphasis may be much the same, although frequently the focus is less upon the atonement as such, and hence the experience is interpreted in a more dif-fuse way. In some circles a double experience is expected:

Christians are those who have been both saved and sanctified, or both born again and baptized by the Holy Spirit with charismata of healing powers, the ability to speak in tongues, and so on. The weakness common to this group of definitions lies not in the importance placed upon the personal experience of divine love, but in the insistence that all valid experiences are uniform to the extent that authenticity can be judged accurately, even severely, by others. The experiential definition of a Christian frequently results in comments such as this about others: "So-and-so is not a Christian because she has not spoken in tongues"; "We are holding a prayer meeting to pray for our pastor, who is not a Christian."

The sociological, doctrinal, ethical, and experiential definitions are not mutually exclusive. Some would insist, for example, that a Christian is one who has had a particular experience, and therefore almost automatically believes certain doctrines and acts in certain ways: "Born-again believers accept the virgin birth of Jesus and his pre-millenial second coming; such persons do not smoke, drink, or dance."

Considering the difficulties inherent in each of the definitions and the way these may be compounded when two or more definitions are joined, the ideal course of action would be to declare a moratorium on the question, "Who is a Christian?" But the question is not likely to go away. Therefore it is well to consider a fifth definition, the one clearly implied in our earlier discussions: "A Christian is one who is baptized."

Properly understood, the fifth definition has no more difficulties than the other four, and has a greater objectivity and integrity than any of them. The proper understanding of this definition must, however, give due weight to both sides of the baptismal covenant. A Christian is one who has been sacramentally claimed and identified by Christ, incorporated into Christ's church, and made a citizen of the new creation. A Christian is also one who throughout life is free to live like a child of God or like a child of the devil. Although given an indelible identity, the Christian is free to ignore the implications of that identity. Thus, to have any real meaning, the term *Christian* requires modifiers when we are speaking from the human side of the covenant: A Christian is either a committed Christian who acts faithfully upon the claims of

Christ, or an uncommitted Christian who ignores or rejects those claims, or a sporadically committed Christian with good intentions but weak performance, and so on.

Awkward though it may be, there is probably no better way of talking about Christians than this double way—who we are from God's perspective, and who we are in terms of our response to what God has done for us. This double way of thinking forces us to separate the question, "Who is a Christian?" from what often appears to be its Siamese twin, "Who will be saved?" When working from the divine side of the covenant, we can answer the first question objectively; and when working from the human side, we may discover some ways of assessing response and commitment, though always these ways will be tentative and recognizably imperfect. But only God is competent to answer the question, "Who will be saved?" There may even be a basic conflict between our desire to have a definite answer to this question and the biblical demand that we live by faith, and not by sight, by trust rather than by proof. It should be sufficient to know that God has both the desire and the capacity to save all.

To some this will appear to be a thinly veiled universalism, or at least a doctrine of eternal security. If God's promises given in baptism are sure, then will not all who are baptized automatically get into heaven? But the matter is not that simple when we take both sides of the covenant seriously. Once more we may take an analogy from our human families. My wife and I are parents of two teen-age daughters. We regard them as members of our family, not merely as preparatory members or partial members. At the moment they confirm this relationship; but there is the possibility that one day they will not, that they will renounce the ways and values of the family, perhaps going even so far as to change their names legally or to disappear so that we cannot locate them. Our children are free to do that if they wish. As many parents have discovered, to their distress, there is no way to prevent such rebellion while maintaining the freedom that is necessary if children are to develop into mature people.

Suppose one of our daughters does say to us, "Look, so far as I am concerned, from here on out I have never heard of you. I don't want to be thought of as your daughter, and I no longer acknowledge you as my family." From her perspective, that may be the case. But can it work the other way around—that we do not want to be thought of as her parents and no longer recognize her as our daughter? No matter what our children may do that is foolish in our eyes, still they are our children. We cannot compel their love; we suffer from the lack of it, and reach out in every possible way to overcome alienation. If this is true in human families, then what of divine love for those who through baptism are proclaimed to be sons and daughters of the Most High God, brothers and sisters in Christ?

To insist on the impossibility of being dropped as members of Christ's family, to assert that in baptism we receive an indelible identity from God in no way infringes upon human freedom, nor does it imply a doctrine of automatic salvation. It does say something about the church's regulations and terminology concerning membership. Of greater importance, it says what must be said about the reliability of God's love, about the responsibility of the community of faith for all of its members, and about the need and motivation to keep and renew the covenant of baptism until death. It reminds us of both the ambiguity and the possibility within that name we use so casually—*Christian.*

# 5

# BUT IS IT BIBLICAL?

Despite the biblical references cited in previous chapters, the understanding of baptism set forth here may seem so novel as to raise the question, "But is it biblical?" The query is legitimate and necessary, primarily because we have almost forgotten how to understand the assumptions the biblical authors took for granted; hence we have lost much of our capacity to think biblically. If this sounds like an exaggerated assertion, it can be supported by looking more closely than usual at key biblical passages related to baptism, and then by examining the biblical viewpoint as it was reflected in early baptismal liturgies.

## DISCOVERING NEW MEANING
## IN KEY BIBLICAL PASSAGES

Examination of all New Testament passages related to baptism would require a separate volume or volumes; but as an example of new meanings we can find in biblical texts when we look at them closely, we shall here consider, first the stories of Jesus' baptism, and then a major segment of the First Letter of Peter. Then we will look briefly at the general biblical view of baptism.

In reading the stories of Jesus' baptism in the Gospels, we tend to see simply interesting accounts surrounding the beginning of our Lord's ministry: he presented himself to John, was baptized, and by the power of the Holy Spirit went forth to overcome temptation and to begin his holy work. But the New Testament writers were not concerned with reporting historical detail; they were determined to convince their readers that Jesus is Messiah. Therefore they are concerned primarily with the identity of Jesus and how he fulfilled the Old Testament hope. Thus in the accounts of the baptism, Jesus is portrayed as the beloved one of God who fulfills and supersedes the prophets.

A careful reading of the baptism narratives reveals that John the Baptizer bears an uncanny resemblence to Elijah, the first of the prophets: both wore shirts of haircloth and leather girdles. Therefore, the reader is to see John as the last of the prophetic era: this is implied in passages such as Matthew 14:5 and Luke 1:17, 76; and it is explicit in Matthew 11:1-15 and Luke 16:16. For the one whom John baptizes inaugurates a new age and establishes a new covenant. The old and the new are not antithetical, however. The new grows out of the old, and may be described in the terms familiar to readers of the Old Testament.

When reading the New Testament, we need to remind ourselves periodically that the writers regarded themselves as devout Jews, and that all they accepted as Scripture was material we call the Old Testament. In particular, the first five books (the *Torah*) were of central importance, and many devout Jews committed much of this material to memory. Converts were expected to make these scriptures their own through concentrated study. Thus, the early Christian authors could allude to Old Testament passages with the expectation that readers would recognize the source and make the necessary connections and interpretations. We have lost that ability for the most part, because we have slighted the study of the Old Testament.

In reading the accounts of the baptism of Jesus we regard the mention of water, the Spirit, and a voice as narrative detail; but the writers intended far more. Genesis 1:1-3 mentions water, the Spirit of God, and the voice of God in conjunction with creation. Specific mention of these three in the Synoptic narratives is intended to point to that fact that Christ is instituting the new creation.[1] What Paul makes explicit with the phrase "new creation" in II Corinthians 5:17 and Galatians 6:15, the Gospel writers present in a more subtle, but equally insistent, way.

It is also important to note that, at the baptism of the Lord, the Spirit is made manifest like a dove. We tend to suppose that the authors simply picked a metaphor according to whim and could as easily have chosen the eagle, about which the Old Testament has many noble things to say. But the choice of the dove was far more deliberate, for it is intended to connect the baptism of Jesus with the story of deliverance in Noah's day. After the deluge, it was a dove that returned with evidence of creation renewed. Jesus has initiated the true new creation and is himself the new ark of salvation. (The relationship between the flood and baptism will become more apparent in our study of I Peter.)

New meaning is also found in the accounts of Jesus' baptism when we begin to explore the motif of Jesus as the new Moses. Matthew makes this connection evident in his birth narrative: Jesus, like the leader of the Exodus, was hidden in Egypt in infancy as protection against the wrath of an ungodly ruler. That this parallel is intended is obvious from Matthew's applying to Jesus a reference that originally applied to Israel and the Exodus—the quotation of Hosea 11:1 in Matthew 2:15, "Out of Egypt have I called my son." In the Synoptic accounts of the temptations that immediately follow Jesus' baptism, what was originally true of Moses is applied to the Lord. After passing through the sea, Moses led his people in the wilderness for forty years, during which time they encountered many temptations. After passing through the water of baptism, Jesus, by going into the wilderness for forty days, recapitulates and brings to fulfillment the experience of Israel. In Matthew's Gospel, the point is quite clear to those who know the Old Testament thoroughly; Jesus is not merely in the wilderness for forty days (as in Mark 1:13 and Luke 4:2) but for "forty days and forty nights"—a phrase borrowed from Exodus 24:18 concerning Moses at Mount Sinai. Thus, Jesus is portrayed as the new Moses who fulfills the Law, and brings a new revelation and covenant from God.[2]

Once we discover the identity of Jesus as the new Moses, his replies to the tempter in the wilderness also take on new significance. Jesus turns back temptation by drawing upon words Moses used in transmitting the Law of God. (Matt. 4:4 and Luke 4:4 = Deut. 8:3; Matt. 4:7 and Luke 4:12 = Deut. 6:16; Matt. 4:10 and Luke 4:8 = Deut. 6:13). Clearly, then,

Jesus through his baptism is revealed as being the leader of the new Exodus and the embodiment of God's *torah*.

For those who have eyes to see it, the accounts of Jesus' baptism have within them all five of the facets of the Gospel discussed in chapter 1. Jesus is the Christ of God who initiates the new covenant and its community, the church; he inaugurates the new creation, the coming kingdom of God. Far from being mere reports of historical detail, the Synoptic accounts of Jesus' baptism are nothing less than proclamations of the gospel in its fullness, yet marvelously condensed in form.

Now we turn to a consideration of crucial passages in I Peter that contain meanings often overlooked. First Peter has usually been regarded as a general, all-occasion letter; until about twenty-five years ago biblical commentaries made almost no mention of baptism in connection with this epistle except when commenting on 3:21, a passage concerning the flood of Noah's time as an anticipation of baptism. Even discussions of that passage were often slight.

More recently it has been suggested that I Peter focuses on baptism and that perhaps it originated as a sermon or tract addressed to the newly baptized, possibly written by Peter in his capacity as bishop, and sent to congregations he could not visit personally when baptisms were being performed. This hypothesis is not universally accepted; but reading the letter with it in mind can enable us to discover much new meaning, particularly in the first three chapters.

If I Peter is addressed to the newly baptized, the meaning of the opening verses becomes more apparent. The new Christians have been "chosen and destined by God the Father and sanctified by the Spirit for obedience to Jesus Christ" (1:2); they "have been born anew to a living hope through the resurrection of Jesus Christ" (1:3). Joy is the keynote of their new life, even in the midst of suffering, which is transient (1:6-9). The newly baptized, having received the fulfillment of the hope of the prophets, are to be obedient children, motivated to holiness of life by the gracious nature and activity of God (1:13-17). Their salvation rests securely upon the saving work of Christ, the unblemished lamb of sacrifice. The language of this section may readily be compared with New Testament passages in which baptism is the explicit concern (e.g., the Trinitarian baptismal language in Matt. 28:19, and the Lamb of God motif in John 1:29-36).

Peter declares that those to whom the letter is addressed have been born anew through the living and abiding word of God preached to them (1:23-25). Having been purified, they are to love one another earnestly from the heart (1:22). As newborn babes, they are to put away all vestiges of the old life and are to grow up to salvation (2:1-3). These statements provide insight into the nature of baptism and its practical fruits.

Twice the readers are referred to as priests (2:5, 9); the second time the author amplifies the meaning by quoting Exodus 19:5-6—the words of Moses concerning the covenant through which the people are made a kingdom of priests and a holy nation. Peter alludes to Genesis 1:3 by writing of "the wonderful deeds of him who called you out of darkness into his marvelous light" (2:9). Then, drawing upon Hosea, Peter affirms what is signified in baptism: "Once you were no people but now you are God's people; once you had not received mercy but now you have received mercy" (2:10).

Having expounded upon the nature of the new life in Christ, Peter turns to concrete ethical implications (addressed perhaps to the entire congregation, not to the newly baptized alone). But periodically in the course of exhortation, the apostle returns to the source of faith—the initiatory activity of God in Jesus Christ (2:21-25; 3:18-4:1a, as well as brief references in chapters 4 and 5).

Particular attention must be given to 3:20-21: "God's patience waited in the days of Noah, during the building of the ark, in which a few, that is, eight persons, were saved through water. Baptism now corresponds to this, not as a removal of dirt from the body but as an appeal to God for a clear conscience, through the resurrection of Jesus Christ." Three points are of particular interest.

(1) Baptism is related to the flood in an emphatic way. We have noted the importance of this in relation to mention of the dove in the narratives of Jesus' baptism.

(2) Baptism is connected intimately with the resurrection of the Lord, that is, with Christ's entrance into the new age in which he exerts dominion. There may be particular meaning

97

in the phrase the RSV renders as "an appeal to God for a clear conscience." Bo Reicke translates the passage thus: Baptism "is a pledge of good will to God. [And it saves you] through the resurrection of Jesus Christ" (brackets his). Reicke believes that underlying the Greek usage here is the idea of a contract confirmed through a solemn procedure of questioning and answering.[3] If he is correct, then we have in I Peter a sacramental theology of the covenant instituted by Christ through the resurrection to which we respond affirmatively—precisely the kind of theology set forth in the first two chapters of this book.

(3) The saved are eight in number. To this third point we are apt to attach no meaning except as it is an incidental detail of the Noah story. Given the Hebraic love of numerology, such an interpretation is naïve, however, for eight was regarded as being a number symbolic of fulfillment and wholeness. The early Christians came to call the day of the Lord's resurrection (the first day of the week) the eighth day of creation. That is, in six days God made the heavens and the earth and everything in them. On the seventh day God rested. On the eighth day, through the resurrection of Christ, God inaugurated the new creation, the age of fulfillment. Those who are baptized live in this eighth day. Furthermore, the number eight signified the assurance of salvation to all who are in Christ. Eight went into Noah's ark, and all of them were saved from destruction. Christ is the new ark of salvation, and all who are in him are secure. It is no accident that since ancient times baptismal pools and fonts have often been made in the shape of an octagon, as many are to this day.

In the last two chapters of the letter, Peter emphasizes the coming kingdom into which the baptized have entered. He speaks of the judgment (4:5-6), and declares that "the end of all things is at hand" (4:7). He refers to "the fiery ordeal" which is coming (4:12) and the internal judgment of the household of God (4:17). He urges watchfulness upon the church, and promises vindication to the faithful (5:6-11).

Thus in I Peter, as in the accounts of Jesus' baptism, we have in connection with Christ and his church, references to creation, covenant, and the coming kingdom in relation to the sacrament of incorporation. When we approach the New

Testament with a new set of eyes, we discover there much to which we have previously been blind. The approach we have been taking to baptism is indeed biblical; but it is seen to be so only after we recognize the assumptions of the authors and look carefully for allusions that readily escape us, particularly if our knowledge of the Old Testament is slight.

A superficial reading of the New Testament sometimes results in the notion that baptism was considered unimportant by the earliest Christians. Paul, in writing to the Corinthians, for example, gave thanks that he had not baptized many there. But a careful reading of I Corinthians 1:13-18 shows this to be an exaltation of the meaning of baptism, not a disparagement of the rite. The Corinthians, having lost sight of the significance of baptism, attached more importance to the person of the minister of baptism than to the unity the sacrament signifies. Paul was grateful he had baptized so few, for otherwise even more would have claimed to be Paul's disciples rather than Christ's new creatures. Paul's allegedly low view of baptism in I Corinthians 1 must be assessed in light of his statements on the subject in Romans 6:1-11 and Galatians 3:27-29. The Romans passage strongly supports the view that baptism is sacramental incorporation into the work of Christ that gives us new life. The statement in Galatians makes unmistakable the equality and unity God's people share through baptismal incorporation.

Because John 4:2 indicates that Jesus himself did not baptize, it is sometimes alleged that he (or at least the writer of the account) gave low priority to the rite. While some scholars view John's Gospel as being non-sacramental, or even anti-sacramental, others hold it to be the most sacramental of all of the Gospels. Certainly John 4:2, like I Corinthians 1:14-15, should be understood as intending to take attention away from the administrator of the sacrament, not from the sacrament itself. Suppose Jesus had baptized some of his followers, who in turn baptized others, and so on through the centuries. Then we would be plagued not only by the claim of some to direct apostolic succession in ordination, but, far worse, by the claim of others to direct dominical succession in baptism; this would destroy the unity baptism proclaims. A careful reading of John indicates that the disciples of Jesus did baptize, apparently with their Lord's approbation.

BAPTISM: CHRIST'S ACT IN THE CHURCH

Even if John's Gospel could without challenge be identified as being anti-sacramental, still the church has the commission to baptize in Matthew 28:19, together with related statements in Luke 24:27 and in the longer ending of Mark; all of these passages point in quite the opposite direction from an allegedly low view of baptism in John. To what extent any of the Gospel passages reflect the thinking of the historical Jesus is, of course, difficult, if not impossible, to ascertain; but they certainly reflect the theology of the early church and the role baptism played in it. Similarly, the numerous reports of baptism in The Acts attest to the importance of initiation rites in the early period of the Christian faith.

It is sometimes asked why the New Testament writers did not report in detail how baptism was performed so that later ages would have clear guidance from the apostolic period. The answer lies in the situation and purpose of the biblical writers. The New Testament authors were evangelists, not chroniclers. Even The Book of the Acts is primarily a proclamation of the faith rather than a history of the church. For the most part, the writers of the New Testament saw no reason to record detailed practices or to offer regulations for a later era; they expected the imminent return of the Lord, and had no inkling there would be a church two thousand years later, let alone that we would be curious about their procedures, or so uneasy about our own as to desire unambiguous directives. The recording of liturgical detail began only after it became evident that history was not ending suddenly in an eschatological crisis.

It is probably by the providence of God that early baptismal practices were not set down in detail; thus, the church is free to develop its own use of the rite under the guidance of the Spirit instead of being bound legalistically to first century specifications. Liturgical legalism is no less a nuisance to the church than is any other form of theological rigidity. Furthermore, a dynamic theology of the Holy Spirit affirms that God will give guidance that is as valuable for our age as that given in the time of the apostles was for their era. Thus, the historical development of initiation practices can be a divine gift. It is not necessarily so, of course. Such development can go far astray—and has over the centuries, as we shall see. But the evolution of practices is not evil in itself;

what is crucial is that the evolving rites be continually checked against biblical understandings of the gospel, as distinct from being confined to liturgical practices clearly attested in the New Testament accounts.

## REFLECTIONS OF BIBLICAL MEANING IN EARLY BAPTISMAL PRACTICES

When the church did get around to recording its initiation practices in some detail, the influence of Scripture upon the rites is evident. To some extent, we may even be able to work our way back to implicit New Testament understandings and practices by looking at the explicit baptismal accounts that emerged after the second century. The literary evidence falls into two great families, the Eastern and Western. The Eastern church came to center around Jerusalem, Antioch, Alexandria, and Constantinople, and is constituted by those bodies we today call the Eastern Orthodox. The Western church centered about Rome, and included North Africa and Italy; in the time of Charlemagne this branch was fused with another centered in France and Spain. The resulting Roman-Frankish rite is the basis of the liturgy of the Roman Catholic Church and the churches of the Reformation, together with their descendants.

Practices varied from time to time and place to place within each tradition and, more particularly, from East to West; the differences were less than we might suppose, however, given the distances and the diversity in language, culture, and theological outlook. We cannot here trace in detail the entire history of baptismal rites. Instead, we shall draw a composite sketch based on ancient practices, relying most heavily upon the Western tradition.

The first writer in the West now known to have described baptism was Justin Martyr, who wrote a defense of the faith around A.D. 160 in an effort to demonstrate to the emperor that Christian liturgical practices, as such, were not dangerous to the state. Because in his time only baptized persons were permitted to attend the portion of the liturgy that began with the intercessions and included sacramental celebration, non-Christians were suspicious about what went on in the secret rites; damaging rumor abounded. Justin wished to set the record straight so that when the state opposed the church it would do so for good reason, not on the basis of misinformation. Justin's account is meager, but it accords well with the next piece of evidence we have in the West, that from the pen of Hippolytus of Rome around A.D. 200.

While the work of Hippolytus is called *The Apostolic Tradition,* to what extent it represents the actual practice of the apostles is difficult to determine. Although he regarded himself as the Bishop of Rome and was canonized after his martyrdom, the Roman Church classified Hippolytus as an anti-pope. He was an arch-conservative, a kind of Bishop Lefebvre of his day, who resisted with might and main new doctrines and practices. Therefore, the liturgies he reported may actually represent the practices of an earlier age, which he was trying to preserve in the face of innovation. Certainly they cannot be regarded as the novelties of a schismatic, for he was a reactionary leader, not a radical one.

The following description of the baptismal process in the ancient church draws heavily upon Hippolytus, but draws upon other sources as well. What is set forth here was generally characteristic of the early centuries, although it does not conform exactly to any one particular set of practices.[4]

During the period we are considering, those interested in embracing the faith were first brought to leaders of the congregation by sponsors who had to vouch for their good lives and serious intention. Certain groups were automatically excluded from the church: prostitutes and pimps, actors, gladiators, and circus performers (because of the unsavory reputation of these amusements at the time), soldiers, and certain government officials (because they were servants of the pagan state and in the course of their duties might be required to take human life in battle or through civil penalties for capital crimes). All who did seek admission to the church were put under careful scrutiny. In part, security dictated this discipline; in times of persecution the church could not risk giving its secrets to those who infiltrated it with a view to subversion. But the scrutiny and discipline of secrecy also stemmed from the conviction that the Christian faith is to be taken with utter seriousness. To be baptized is to be called into a life of grateful, obedient service to God.

Prospective Christians studied under careful direction for three years; while attendance at worship was expected during this time, the unbaptized were allowed to be present only for the reading of the Scriptures and the sermon, after which they were dismissed. They could not pray with the congregation, for they were not yet joined to it by Christ. Nor could they come to the Lord's Table, for they were not yet members of his body. This long period of preparation we call the catechumenate (related to our word *catechism*, meaning instruction).

At the end of three years, catechumens were admitted by vote of the congregation to the final stage of preparation for baptism, which took place during the season we know as Lent. During this time, they engaged in intensive study, prayer, and fasting, and were taught the Creed and the Lord's Prayer, which hitherto had been kept from them as belonging only to the church. The candidates for baptism submitted to repeated rites of exorcism, intended to release them from the power of the devil; these rites included practices such as breathing into the face of the candidates, anointing them with oil, and making the sign of the cross upon them.

The principal rites of baptism began before dawn on Easter Day. During the night the congregation and candidates gathered for a vigil service that included the reading of scripture from the Old Testament about the story of salvation. At daybreak the candidates, sponsors, and clergy gathered at a stream (or later, in a baptistry). At some point before the administration of water, a prayer was offered, recounting God's destructive-creative use of water in the history of salvation and asking for the work of the Holy Spirit.

In some places, the candidates came barefoot, and wore rough clothing (perhaps of animal hair). But soon they stripped naked. Three times they explicitly renounced Satan, and were anointed with the oil of exorcism. For this procedure they sometimes faced west, and turned to face east following it. They then went down into the water, making a statement of adherence to Christ. Next followed an interrogation consisting of three questions, each answered with the words, "I believe."

The questions as given in *The Apostolic Tradition* are recognizable to us as the antecedents of the Apostles' Creed:

Do you believe in God the Father Almighty?

Do you believe in Christ Jesus, the Son of God, who was born of Holy Spirit and the Virgin Mary, who was crucified in the days of Pontius Pilate, and died, and rose the third day living from the dead, and ascended into heaven, and sat down at the right hand of the Father, and will come to judge the living and the dead?

Do you believe in the Holy Spirit, in the Holy Church, and the resurrection of the flesh?

After each response, water was administered. Hippolytus notes that infants and children were baptized first, with parents or other family members making the responses for those too young to answer for themselves. Then adults were baptized. Normally, either the bishop or presbyters (elders) were the ministers of baptism, assisted by deacons. Because candidates were nude, women deacons sometimes accompanied female candidates, with the male clergy standing at a discreet distance to ask the questions.

Upon coming out of the water, the new Christians were again anointed, and were given a fresh, white garment to wear—and perhaps shoes as well. They may also have been given a lighted candle. Thus furnished, they went in procession to rejoin the worshiping congregation. In the liturgical assembly, the bishop held his hands over the heads of the initiates, and prayed for them. Then he poured upon their heads a specially prepared oil known as chrism, or myron, and placed his hand on their heads, tracing the sign of the cross on their foreheads with his thumb. Now, for the first time, the bishop greeted the new members of the church with the traditional gesture of reconciliation and love, the kiss of peace. With the exchange of the peace, the entire congregation welcomed the new Christians to the Table of the Lord. In addition to the bread and wine of the Eucharist, the new members were sometimes given a cup of milk and honey. The service concluded with great joy and thanksgiving.

During the week following, the new Christians came to

church daily to be instructed in the meaning of the rites they had experienced.[5] During this week, the neophytes wore their new white robes, and refrained from the daily bath that was customary in that culture.

Thus, the early Christians were baptized. While we now think of baptism as being simply the administration of water as part of a brief liturgy, in their time baptism was a process extending over a considerable period of time. One evidence of this is the fact that a catechumen who died before receiving the bath of water was nevertheless entitled to Christian burial rites. Only after several centuries did baptism come to be thought of in the restricted sense common to our day.

Contemporary Christians, particularly Protestants, may recoil in dismay from a process that to us seems incredibly complex, perhaps even unbiblical. From the Puritans we have inherited extreme simplicity in worship, particularly with respect to ceremonies. From the revivalists we have a legacy of spontaneity in worship. Both of these we have tended to read back into the New Testament approach to liturgy. But both Judaism and the pagan cults, from which converts came to the Christian faith, accepted complex rites, filled with tradition and symbolism. That people, upon becoming Christian, should suddenly reject the kinds of practices they had valued since childhood is hardly likely; our suppositions to the contrary betray an unrealistic view of human nature.

Furthermore, we need to re-examine our assumption that simplicity and spontaneity more fully reflect biblical faith than do rites that are carefully thought out and filled with symbolic action. We cannot be certain to what extent the practices from the third century onward were the practices of the apostolic age, but when we look at the matter closely, we discover that, in fact, they reflect apostolic ideas and images. To this extent, at least, the rites were biblical in spirit. Therefore, we turn now to look at the meanings drawn from Scripture that the early Christians incorporated into their baptismal practices.

We are likely to be alienated from the ancient rites at the very outset by the exorcisms. Exorcism is hardly an unknown word to a generation that has read a novel and seen a celebrated movie about it; but the practice is mystifying to us, and the assumptions behind it may even be offensive. We like to think that we have outgrown notions of demonic possession. Yet the Bible accepts such notions. Whatever problems we may have with the accounts of Jesus' exorcisms, our attempts to explain them away with contemporary psychological jargon may be more naïve than we consider the accounts themselves to be. At least the New Testament takes seriously the pervasiveness and persistence of sin. It admits that there is evil in our world that simply does not submit to solutions based upon increased education or financial outlay. The early Christians understood what post-enlightenment rationalists tend to ignore—that sometimes those who have the most learning or wealth seem to be gripped most tightly in the clutches of evil, and that sin is so entrenched that it cannot be driven out except by divine power.

The practice of breathing upon the catechumen (and later, of breathing over the baptismal water) was a reminder of God's activity in struggling against chaos; for in Genesis 1:2 God's breath (wind) moves over the waters. The rite of breathing (technically called insufflation) also represents God's creation of Adam, and Christ's inauguration of the new creation by breathing upon his disciples on the evening of the resurrection and saying to them, "Receive the Holy Spirit" (Gen. 2:7; John 20:22).

The realism of the New Testament in acknowledging the power of evil (though hardly of a red devil with horns, pitchfork, and pointed tail) was also evident in the way candidates came to their baptism. In ancient cultures, slaves were not permitted to wear shoes. Thus, by coming barefoot, candidates acknowledged that they were slaves to sin (John 8:34-35). They wore the rough clothing of repentance, as did John the Baptizer; God clothed Adam and Eve with animal hides, and the candidates came as children of the old creation, awaiting the work of the New Adam who gives life (Gen. 3:21; I Cor. 15:45).

The early Christians knew that the ways of Satan must be renounced emphatically and repeatedly. Thus, the candidates made three renunciations, accompanied, perhaps, by spitting as a sign of defiance of the devil. The triple renunciation balanced the triple affirmation of faith in God the Father, Son, and Holy Spirit; and the number three had sacred connotations in the numerology of the time. When candidates faced west for the renunciations, and turned eastward for the statement of adherence to Christ and for the triple affirmation, this was a symbolic turning from darkness to light. The west, being the direction of sunset, was associated with the power of evil; but Christ is the dawn (Luke 1:78-79), the sun of righteousness that rises with healing in its wings (Mal. 4:2), the light of the world (John 8:12), whose very nativity was heralded by a star in the east (Matt. 2:2). The early Christians expected that, at his return, Christ would appear in the east, extending his dominion unto the west (Matt. 24:27). It was common for early Christians to face the east when at prayer—not, as is sometimes supposed, to face the holy city (as Jews turned toward Jerusalem, and Muslims later came to face Mecca), but to acknowledge the Light of the World and to look for his appearing in glory.

The timing of the ancient baptismal rite at daybreak on the occasion of Passover was also important. It was thought that the Lord would come in glory at night, thereby asserting his triumph over the demonic powers of darkness, and that he would return at the same time of the year that he had arisen from the dead. Therefore, Christians gathered annually to keep vigil, should their Lord return during that Pasch. But when the break of day made it apparent that they would have to wait for at least another year, the faithful did not disperse in dismay or disappointment. Instead, they shared sacramentally in the coming kingdom they knew themselves to be a part of already. The candidates were incorporated into the eschatological reality through baptism; then all of the faithful shared in the eucharistic foretaste of the great feast of the kingdom in heaven, the city of light.

All of this, together with the giving of a lighted candle to the newly baptized in some rites, recalls the New Testament practice of calling Christians "the enlightened ones" (Heb. 6:4, 10:32; Eph. 1:18), as well as the words of Jesus that his disciples are the light of the world (Matt. 5:14-16). Justin Martyr, and others after him, referred to baptism itself as enlightenment.

The church saw several meanings associated with renunciation and affirmation in the act of stripping and entering the water naked. This represented putting off the old nature and returning to the original innocence of Adam and Eve in the garden. It was also an identification with the Incarnation, for Jesus had come into the world naked from the water of Mary's womb. The donning of new garments upon emerging from the water represented the putting on of Christ in baptism (Gal. 3:27; Col. 3:9-14).

Probably the portion of the ancient baptismal rite that strikes us as being most natural and familiar is that of washing with water. Obviously it signified the washing away of sin (Acts 2:38; I Cor. 6:11, Eph. 5:26; and Heb. 10:22, which is typological in fulfillment of Lev. 16:4). But there is more to washing than the basically negative act of eliminating impurity.

Washing also has a very positive meaning in the New Testament. The letter to Titus, in language which is undeniably baptismal, refers to "the washing of regeneration and renewal in the Holy Spirit which [God] poured out upon us richly through Jesus Christ our Savior so that we might be justified by his grace and become heirs in hope of eternal life" (3:5-7). The phrase *washing of regeneration* may well reflect the ancient connection between water and life. The fact that the human fetus comes forth from the womb with water made this association inescapable among primitive peoples. In Genesis 1:20, the first animals are those which swarm in the water. (We have been taught that the early designation of Christ as ICHTHUS [fish] was an acrostic for the affirmation "Jesus Christ, God's Son, Savior"; what we have not often been told is that the sign of the fish was also a reminder that through the water of baptism Christians become the first living creatures of the New Creation.) In Noah's day, the earth was not only cleansed of sin, but was also regenerated by being washed with water.

There may well be a combination of the baptismal images of enlightenment, robing, and regeneration in the otherwise strange comment of Revelation 7:14 concerning the multitude of the redeemed: "They have washed their robes and made them white in the blood of the Lamb." Perhaps we are so accustomed to references in sermons and hymns about being washed in the blood of the Lamb that we fail to see how utterly unlikely it is that dirty fabric should be cleansed by dipping it in blood. Probably the author meant something quite different and more important than that. First, blood represents life. The shedding of Christ's blood was not primarily a way of paying a price for sin (a negative action) but a means by which the world can be infused with the divine life poured out upon it. Classical artists understood this when they depicted beneath the cross the skull and bones of Adam, whose sinful race was revivified by the atoning work of Christ. Second, the word translated as *white* means more than is obvious. Particularly when used in an eschatological context, this term means "radiant with light." It is the same word used of Jesus at his transfiguration, of the angel at the empty tomb, and of the radiance of Christ in Revelation 1:14.[6] Finally, in the code language of eschatological writings, clothing stands not merely for apparel but for the very being of the person thus clothed. To those who understand Revelation 7:14 in this deeper way, the giving of the white garment at baptism signifies that those washed with the sacramental water receive the life of Christ, and put on the radiance of his glory in the new age.

The numerous anointings associated with baptism in the early centuries may puzzle us. We are helped to understand them by knowing that in the ancient world anointing was bound up with the act of bathing; oil was used much as we use soap and skin lotion. As the water of the daily bath took on new meaning in baptism, so also did the oil of familiar practice. Scripture connects oil with both Christ and the Holy Spirit. The terms *messiah* and *christ* are the Hebrew and Greek designations (respectively) meaning "the anointed one." Behind this image lies the Hebrew tradition of anointing kings and priests at their investiture. Thus messiah-christ is the King of kings and the great High Priest; through baptism, he incorporates us into himself so that we become members of his kingdom, his priestly people (I Peter 2:5, 9; Rev. 1:5-6).

Oil is particularly associated with the Holy Spirit. We have noted that the dove in the narratives of Jesus' baptism is reminiscent of the dove of Noah's ark. The dove in Noah's day revealed the beginning of the renewal of the earth by bringing back an olive branch, an ancient symbol of peace. Isaiah 61:3 and Psalm 45:7 speak of the oil of gladness; this, coupled with the opening words of Isaiah 61 ("The Spirit of the Lord God is upon me, because the Lord has anointed me . . . "), makes it understandable that oil should be a sign of the joy of the Spirit, and also of the power of the Spirit given to those sent into mission (for it was Isaiah 61 Jesus read from at the inauguration of his ministry in Nazareth). At this and other points, the relationship of messiah, (the anointed one), and the Spirit (the one who anoints) is established in such a way as to make necessary some ambiguity in the significance of anointing.

Anointing is thus a uniquely apt reminder of the unity of Christ and of the Spirit in the Christian life. To be bound to one through baptism is to be bound to both, and to receive the blessings of both. This is particularly clear in the Johannine writings. In I John 2:27, the author observes: "The anointing which you received from him [Christ, the anointed one] abides in you" and "his anointing teaches you everything." From the words concerning the Spirit in chapters 14 and 15 of John's Gospel, we know that it is the Spirit who abides in us and teaches us. Anointing affirms the unity of Christ and the Holy Spirit whose work is one.

The making of the sign of the cross on the forehead was associated with the anointing by the bishop in the early rites. This action is known by several technical terms: signation, consignation, chrismation, sealing, and the *sphragis* (Greek term for *seal*). The final two designations reveal the deep metaphorical meaning of the act.

A seal is an identifying mark that indicates authenticity. Documents of importance are given a seal. We are familiar with the Great Seal of the United States and with the seal of its President. Notaries Public affix seals to attest legality. In ancient times, letters and wills were sealed by an insignia stamped into warm wax. For this purpose, signet rings were made and were closely guarded, being worn on one's person, lest they fall into the possession of someone not authorized to use them. The seal is mentiond in Ephesians 1:13-14 and II Corinthians 1:22, where it is called an "earnest" or guarantee of our inheritance. Ephesians 4:20 mentions sealing in the Spirit; and in II Timothy 2:19, the seal is related to identity and ownership—and therefore to protection. The connotations of sealing as a part of baptism are rich indeed.

The biblical basis for an identifying mark related to God's care is well established from the beginning of the Old Testament. Cain is given such a mark (Gen. 4:15). The Israelites in Egypt marked their doors with the blood of the paschal lamb in order that the angel of death might pass over them (Exod. 12:7, 12-13). In Ezekiel 9:4-6, the prophet is instructed to mark the foreheads of the righteous as protection against destruction. Even the idea of God as shepherd relates indirectly to the seal; for sheep were branded in order to prevent their loss or theft.

The seal on the forehead at baptism connects the baptized one with Christ, not only because *christ* means *anointed*, but also because the insignia made with the oil has a double christological meaning. The sign of the cross in its Greek form is employed; this indicates even more the importance of our incorporation into Jesus' death. The Greek cross, having four arms of equal length, is an "x" turned on its side; thus it is also an abbreviation for XPISTOS, the Greek form of *christ*. Signation is a reminder that the newly baptized is incorporated into the Lord's death, and is also given the Lord's own name.

As if this were not sufficient symbolic richness for a single act, the name of Christ imposed on the forehead at baptism was related to the fact that Christians frequently assumed new names of their own at baptism. Those coming from pagan religions were particularly urged to change their names and to assume the names of biblical persons, or of Christians of previous generations.

All of this helps us understand baptismal allusions in The Revelation. The apocalyptic writer speaks about those who have been sealed on their foreheads (7:3, 9:4). This seal is the name of Christ (14:1), a new name (2:17; 3:12). The author of The Revelation takes the idea of the identifying mark on the forehead from Ezekiel 9:4-6, where the term usually translated *mark* is identical with the name of the last letter of the Hebrew alphabet—*tau*. While changes in orthography have caused *tau* to bear no resemblance to "x" or " + ," the letter originally had the cruciform shape, as is shown in coins of the Maccabean period. Thus, Ezekiel was instructed to mark the heads of the righteous with a cross (the Jerusalem Bible so translates the Hebrew). Then, of course, this figure had no relationship to the instrument of execution in the Roman empire; but it was (as it is now among illiterate peoples) an identifying mark having the status of a signature. Hence, it was God's mysterious name which Ezekiel was to place upon the foreheads of the righteous, for the final letter of the Hebrew alphabet carried the same meanings of transcendence and eternity that the *omega* of the Greek alphabet assumed in the New Testament. The author of The Revelation saw profound typological implications in the Ezekiel text and made the most of them. It may even be that he saw priestly significance in the sign; according to the *Talmud,* the priests of Israel were anointed with the sign of *tau.* It is difficult to know whether the author of The Revelation read meaning into baptismal signation, or whether the Christian community already understood all of these meanings to be implied in the sign of the cross. It is clear that when later generations employed the cross at the time of signation, they were able to draw upon a multiplicity of biblical meanings. For these Christians, the apparently simple act of tracing upon the forehead the form " + " had immense importance as a sign of participation in the eternal kingdom of Christ by the power of the Holy Spirit.

The laying on of hands also was rich in meaning. In the Old Testament, this action is associated with the commissioning of leaders and the ordaining of priests (Num. 27:18, 8:10), as well as with blessing and the offering of sacrifice (Gen. 48:14; Exod. 29:10). In the New Testament, the laying on of hands came to be associated with healing and reconciliation, as well as with ordination. All of these meanings are important in baptism. Through the sacrament, Christ heals his people from the disease of sin, reconciling them to God and one another, and offering them the blessings of eternal life; the baptized are ordained and commissioned to serve as priests in Christ's kingdom, and as living oblations, who render to God the sacrifice of obedience and praise.

The cup of sweetened milk, sometimes given to the newly baptized, was related to the frequent Old Testament appellation for Canaan—the land of milk and honey. Furthermore, it is natural to refer in symbolic terms to milk as the diet of the newborn. This I Peter 2:2-3 does; in I Corinthians 3:2 and Hebrews 5:12-13 milk is also mentioned in relation to spiritual infancy (although pejoratively in both cases, since the writers are prodding Christians to seek more solid food, as befits the mature). Milk and honey particularly bring Exodus imagery into play, for Canaan was the goal of the refugees from Egypt.

We must now connect this with the primary occasion for baptism in the ancient church.

The normal time for baptism was the season of Easter. The most favored occasion was the vigil that opens the season, and we have already seen that this day was originally related to the expectation of the Lord's return in glory. Easter, was, however, a season of fifty days, in accordance with the Jewish observance of time from the Day of Passover to the day of Pentecost. In the church, the concluding day of this period became the second-most favored day for baptism, reserved for those who could not be present at the Easter Vigil. (Not until the fourth century did the Day of Pentecost begin to develop into a distinct day that eventually celebrated the coming of the Holy Spirit in power and sometimes was seen as inaugurating a new liturgical season. In the early centuries, the entire fifty days commemorated the unitary action of Christ in his passion, death, resurrection, and formation of the church by the power of the Spirit. The first and final days of the "Great Fifty" were liturgical brackets for a season of unusual importance and joy.)

To be baptized during Easter, particularly on its opening or closing day, was to celebrate the Christian Pasch, release under the New Moses from bondage to sin and death, and formation as the church, the new Israel of God. By virtue of the very occasion, Christians could confess that "we were buried therefore in baptism into his death, so that as Christ was raised from the dead by the glory of the Father, we too might walk in newness of life" (Rom. 6:3-4). While provision was made for baptism at other times in cases of necessity, the ancient church knew nothing of the contemporary practice of scheduling baptism at the convenience of the candidates. Reports in The Acts of baptism performed on the spot without a congregation present (the Ethiopian eunuch, the Philippian jailer, Saul of Tarsus, and others) reflect a unique missionary situation and the theological purposes of Luke. They do not represent the norm of the ancient church, and still less do they serve as mandates for the practice of the church today. For the early Christians, timing had a significance that complemented the other symbolic aspects of initiation.

Questions are raised in the contemporary mind by the final initiation practice of the ancient church, that of coming to worship daily wearing the new white robes throughout the week following baptism, and that of refraining from the customary daily bath during this period. First about the bath: abstinence from bathing was not a rejection of cleanliness, nor did it result from superstitious belief that the residue of water and oil from baptism must remain on the skin as long as possible. Rather, it sprang from factors related to the daily bath itself. Such a bath was a source of relaxation and pleasure, and normally took place in a public bath house in the company of other people from the community. Abstaining for a week was a reminder that true joy is found in the kingdom of Christ, in his purity and the richness of his Spirit. The true community of the Christian is the church, which, although it is always in the world, is never entirely of the world.

The week following Easter day had a particular significance; for the Jews, the observance of Passover inaugurated the seven days of unleavened bread, a special period of solemnity. Thus, it was natural for the early Christians to find heightened meaning in the seven days following the celebration of the resurrection. Nor can the importance of numbers be overlooked. The Lord's saving action, celebrated on Easter day, inaugurates the eighth day of creation, the new age of Christ. So Easter day itself inaugurates a time of eight days (an octave) of particular significance, during which new Christians wear their new clothes as a sign of their participation in the new creation.

The daily worship of the newly baptized was a way of pointing toward the continual renewal baptism demands. Having received the water, the anointing and consignation, the milk and honey, and the bread and wine, the new Christians were not to suppose that they had completed the journey begun more than three years earlier. Rather, they had embarked upon a journey of faith that calls for daily devotion and study, constant commitment to the challenge of walking in that newness of life Christ imparts. In baptism, the new Christians took up the cross in an impressive sacramental way; now they would need to take up the cross daily in a very practical way if they were to keep and renew their baptism until death.

This, then, was the form and meaning of the ancient

initiation process. While we cannot be certain how many of the practices employed in the early centuries actually go back to apostolic times, we can see that the practices, regardless of the time of their origin as liturgical acts, reflect biblical thinking and imagery. It is our inability to read the Scriptures imaginatively that sometimes leads us to think that the early practices were inventions of an unbiblical kind, or even importations from paganism.

Once we learn to read the Bible in a new way, we are confronted with the question, "Which of the ancient practices, if any, should we reinstitute as a way of proclaiming the biblical faith in our time?" Interesting as that query may be, an attempt to answer it is premature. A more pertinent question demands our immediate attention: "Given the richness and complexity of early Christian initiation, how did we get from that to a perfunctory sprinkling of a few drops of water upon someone during a Sunday morning preaching service—or even in private?" To put it another way, the early Christians regarded baptism as being of central importance in their Christian experience. Today, baptism is often looked upon as an activity of minor importance with little relationship either to the real world or to the life of faith. So what went wrong?

# 6

# WHAT WENT WRONG?

It is evident that since the early centuries something has gone awry. The difficulty is not merely that the church came to interpret baptism in different ways; for in each age, the Christian community must wrestle with the deep meaning of the biblical faith and seek to communicate it in an idiom the current generation can grasp and appreciate. This necessarily involves a certain amount of change. We are confronted here with something more complex. The rich meaning of baptism found in the New Testament and in the early church has virtually been lost in many quarters, and the attempt to communicate the faith through baptism has been all but given up. Why?

## THE BACKGROUND TO THE CHANGE

In order to understand the changes that occurred in later eras, it is helpful to summarize the early understanding of worship and the role of the ministers in it, for this will provide a crucial contrast with developments in subsequent centuries.

In early Christian thought, worship was the godly work of the entire Christian community, and what occurred in the liturgy was seen in the context of a dynamic view of time. From Judaism the church inherited the conviction that, in worship, the acts of God already accomplished in history are called again into the community's experience and that the acts of God promised in the future are already enjoyed by the faithful in an anticipatory way. Thus the past, present, and future are inextricably linked, though not fused.

While we have lost this understanding to a large degree, even in the Lord's Supper, there at least it is still retained sufficiently for the Eucharist to serve as a helpful illustration. When we come to the Lord's Table, we are gathered at a particular geographical location at a specific time in the history of the world. Yet we are not prisoners of time and space. When we unite with our Lord around his table, we also call into our present experience his meals on the hillsides with his followers, the supper in the upper room on the night he was betrayed and arrested, his supper at Emmaus on the evening of his resurrection, and the countless Eucharists shared by the faithful across the ages. Furthermore, as we share in the meal of bread and wine, we anticipate the great heavenly banquet that marks the fulfillment of the Lord's redemptive work; already we participate in the joy of the saints who are gathered about the table at the great feast of grace.

Seen in this perspective, liturgical time is rich in meaning and fluid. It is impossible to pinpoint one particular act within the liturgy as being "it." The whole of worship puts the entire contemporary community of faith in touch with all of reality—past, present, and future. This is the early understanding of things; to have asked the Christians of the first centuries, "At what one point in your worship does God enter in a unique way?" would probably have been to receive a vacant, uncomprehending stare. In contrast to later understanding, baptism was a process that extended over a period of time and possessed a unity within itself and in relation to the whole of the Christian faith; baptism was connected to everything in the Christian life.

The worshiping congregation also possessed a vital unity. One of its members was designated presiding minister (bishop); deacons assisted. But all members of the congregation were involved in the liturgical action; they were not spectators. As head of the local community, the bishop had responsibility for maintaining and teaching the doctrines of the apostles, and for overseeing the community and its worship. But the notion that bishops had special powers granted to them by God without reference to the community of faith would have been so foreign to early Christian thinking as to be incomprehensible. As the congregation could not function without a bishop, so a bishop could not function without a congregation. But the latter part of this equation became less and less evident throughout the centuries, until finally it seemed to have no importance at all.

In order to comprehend changes in the understanding of baptism in later ages, we need also to look at the early Christian understanding of sin and grace. Here, too, the view of things was fluid and dynamic. The reality of sin was tied to the reign of evil in the world. To be a sinner was to be under the domination of evil, to be submissive to its power. But Christ, in his saving work, inaugurated in our midst the kingdom of righteousness, thereby cancelling the ultimate power of evil and opening to us the dominion of grace. Through baptism we renounce allegiance to the old order, which we know to be doomed even though it still makes pretensions of power. We proclaim allegiance to Christ, and by God's goodness (grace) we are incorporated into the Lord's kingdom.

This does not mean that suddenly we no longer commit any sinful act, or that we have no wrong desires. But we no longer give ultimate allegiance to these; they cease to be our idols. When we sin, it is an act contrary to our true loyalty, and the transgression is covered by the atoning work of Christ. An absolute fall from grace may be possible, but it requires an explicit renunciation of Christ and his kingdom, and a deliberate embracing of the old order when one knows it to be doomed. We do not fall from grace simply through weakness. On the other hand, we cannot use weakness as an excuse to avoid all opportunities to do what is right. Grace involves being placed within the dominion of Christ and his sanctifying power. Salvation is more than being moved into neutral territory. We are saved unto good works, even though we are not saved by good works.

Thus grace, like time, was understood in a non-rigid way by the early Christians. A later and more static interpretation of the nature of sin and salvation would depart from this in crucial ways, and thus would alter significantly the church's understanding of baptism.

In order to comprehend what went wrong concerning the understanding of baptism over the centuries, it is helpful to note two phenomena that contribute to the problem of misinterpretation. First, practices that arise for one reason will often be perpetuated for a quite different reason. Second, in the midst of a heated controversy, it is often necessary to make a strong affirmation, which, when the battle has been won, comes to be understood in a very different way, in a way that has consequences unforeseen in the original situation. These two tendencies interact; many times, new reasons for perpetuating old practices are derived from a point of controversy that comes to be understood differently once the dispute itself has subsided. The impact of this interaction can be exceedingly destructive, as we will have ample opportunity to observe.

## THE PROCESS OF DETERIORATION
## BEFORE THE REFORMATION

While there is no clear evidence on the subject in the New Testament, it is evident that, by the close of the second century, infants and children were being baptized, as Hippolytus noted. Probably this practice arose out of a strong sense of community and of the importance of nurture within that community. Children within the covenant family were seen to be members of it, not aliens; when they understood themselves to be partakers of the covenant, they were better able to respond to God's grace and to resist the lure of Satan's pretended domination. Ultimately, therefore, baptism was connected with sin and its remission; but the effect of baptism upon sin was not pinpointed to the moment of the administration of the sacrament.

Gradually, however, Christians lost their Jewish heritage, with its healthy tolerance of liturgical and theological ambiguity. Particularly in the West, the church fell heir to the legal tradition of the Roman empire, and the attendant love of precision in word and action. Further, the rise of faith coincided with the decline of that empire; usually a civilization that is threatened with collapse seeks to allay its anxiety by becoming even more precise and rigid. (Someone has observed that the last thing a dying institution does is to issue a formidable code of picayune regulations.) Those facing the disintegration of their empire and its culture needed a very stable formulation of their faith.

Thus, as the sense of corporateness and openness in theology and worship declined, the baptism of infants came to be justified for a new set of reasons—infants are born under the curse of sin; baptism is related to sin and its remission. Therefore, the church must baptize infants in order to spare them the awful consequences of this curse. A practice begun for one set of reasons (assumptions about the corporate nature of the community of faith) is continued for quite another set of reasons (assumptions about sin and its remission).

This instance of the first tendency at work is complicated when the second tendency is added as a result of the Pelagian heresy of the fifth century. Pelagius had a very generous view of human nature and argued that sin is but the conscious and deliberate violation of God's law. Because it involves only conscious acts, sin is not a characteristic of infants. Furthermore, it may be possible for some people to avoid sin altogether. In reaction, Augustine, the preeminent theologian of the age, said what had to be said: sin is all-pervasive and totally seductive. We are not so much sinners because we want to be or intend to be, as because we cannot help ourselves. We are born under the dominion of sin and may be totally blind to its power over us. Each of us, said Augustine, is born with the stain of Adam upon us; and so damning is that stain that there is no possibility of a sinless life. Therefore, salvation is from God alone.

Augustine was involved in another controversy that would influence later understanding of baptism also, this one with the Donatists, who insisted that a sacrament is properly administered only if the minister of it is morally pure. A number of dangers were inherent in the Donatist position. Who is to define, let alone judge, what constitutes moral purity? Because all are sinners, both the accused and the accuser are infected by the same disease, even if in different stages of development. And how does one distinguish moral judgment from subjective preference? One potential recipient of a sacrament may refuse reception because of first-hand knowledge that the minister has committed murder; but other potential recipients may refuse the ministry of others because of the color of their hair, or because they liked the way the previous pastor did things better—all the while covering their subjective dislike with some "moral" pretext. Above all, how can one say that the sacrament is an activity of God, if God is bound by the character of the minister? In this controversy, too, Augustine said what had to be said: Rites are true sacraments when they are administered by those whom the church has authorized, quite apart from the moral character of the particular minister.[1]

Augustine's positions in relation to the Pelagians and the Donatists were accepted by the church for good reason. But once the controversies subsided, these positions came to be understood differently. In the centuries after Augustine, sin and baptism came to be interpreted more and more mechanically until, by the late middle ages, there emerged an understanding quite alien to the perspective of the early church. Sin came to be divided into two categories: original (which each human being inherits at birth from Adam) and actual (which each person commits during youth and adulthood). Baptism removes the original guilt—and would remove the guilt of actual sin, were it not so risky to wait until late in life to be baptized. (When this understanding was emerging, but before it came to its rigid final form, some people did delay baptism until they were on their deathbeds.) The threat of unexpected death in adulthood and the high infant mortality rate both militated against taking unwarranted risks; baptism must be administered soon after birth. But with the antidote for sin administered in infancy, what was to be done about the guilt attached to actual sin? For this purpose there arose a system of penance during adulthood.[2]

Thus, baptism came to be administered to infants for reasons quite different from those that obtained in the early centuries; and Augustine's statements about the universality of sin and the objectivity of the sacrament came to be understood in new ways once the controversies that necessarily produced them had been put to rest. The early ideas about baptism and its practice deteriorated slowly over centuries.

There were related problems that exacerbated the deterioration. In the ancient church, the prayer that was said over the water on each occasion of baptism was an act of thanksgiving to God. But it came to be viewed as a means of conferring special blessing upon the water; and because of the objectivity of the sacrament, such water once blessed was regarded as being holy. Thus, water blessed at the Easter Vigil was not disposed of at the close of the liturgy, but was retained in the font for use again (without another prayer of blessing) at the end of the Easter season. The practice degenerated into superstition. People came into the churches to steal some of the "holy" water for medicinal purposes, for use as an aphrodisiac, or even to make tastier gravies and sauces. Finally, covers that could be secured by locks had to be devised for baptismal fonts.

(Lest we sneer at such superstition as being a medieval oddity, we do well to consider an incident that occurred in American Protestantism in the second half of the twentieth century. After their child was baptized, the parents requested that the water in the font be given them to take home. When the bewildered pastor inquired as to the reason, they replied, "We will keep it in a sealed bottle; if our child is ever critically ill, we will rub her with it." The incident is more typical than we care to admit.)

Practical matters also producd changed perceptions of the meaning of baptism. One such matter had to do with the authority of bishops. Whereas once every city had a bishop who presided over the worship in that place, eventually episcopal jurisdiction was greatly extended to include large territories or tribes. Then the bishop could not be present at every baptism, and the authority to baptize had to be extended to lesser clerics. One particular action in the baptismal process created special problems, however. The signation with chrism, instead of being viewed as a liturgical function of the bishop in the capacity of presiding officer, came to be regarded as the conferring of a special kind of grace. No longer was the minister acting on behalf of the congregation in the name of God, but was acting by direct authority from God apart from the congregation. So who had this authority in the matter of chrismation?

The Eastern churches solved the dilemma by allowing priests to administer chrismation at the time of baptism, using oil consecrated by a bishop. But in the West, this permission was not extended to priests. In many cases, therefore, chrismation by a bishop was delayed for a long period of time after the administration of the water by a priest. Some attempts were made to retain the ancient traditions. The baptism of infants was to be at Easter and at Pentecost, except in cases where the death of the child seemed imminent; on these major festivals the bishop could preside in one of the principal churches of the diocese. Nor were baptisms to be conducted in every parish church, but only at a limited number of sites so that the baptized would have a sense of community related to a common baptismal font. The custom of having a baptismal font in every church developed only gradually. But attempts to continue the traditions were not successful over the long haul, and baptism came to be administered on any occasion and in any church—often with both bishop and congregation absent. Laws were enacted compelling parents to have their infants baptized within a specified number of days after birth, and thus the preeminence of Easter Day and the Day of Pentecost as baptismal occasions waned. It should come as no surprise that the conscious connection between baptism and incorporation into the paschal mystery also declined.

Because the interval between baptism and the visit of the bishop was quite long in many cases, parents were apathetic about bringing children for chrismation. Therefore, theologians eventually sought to find reasons that would encourage chrismation and that would even justify the gap between the two ceremonies. Hence, chrismation, once an integral part of the baptismal process, came to be regarded as an independent sacrament known as confirmation, not merely as the result of the unfortunate delay in the completion of the baptismal rite.

Three general types of justification for confirmation as a separate rite arose: (1) Baptism, it was said, is incomplete in itself; it is completed only by confirmation, in which the seal of the Holy Spirit is conferred upon what was done earlier. (2) While Christians do receive the Holy Spirit in baptism, in order to do battle with sin they need the strengthening power of the Spirit that is given at confirmation. (3) While Christians do receive the Holy Spirit in baptism, there are special gifts of the Spirit that are conferred at confirmation in order that the baptized may fulfill their ministry as members of the church. The first rationale most clearly depreciates baptism, but all three tend to demean it by insisting upon the need for another sacrament. This diminution of the meaning of baptism reduces it to little more than an antidote for original sin. Such a constricted interpretation of baptism had vast and unfortunate implications.

The theological importance attached to a delayed rite of episcopal anointing made it imperative that parents present children for confirmation. But how could compliance be insured? In England in 1281, the Council of Lambeth ordered that thereafter unconfirmed persons could not receive communion. The intention was not to keep people away from the Eucharist, but rather to guarantee confirmation by imposing a penalty of great magnitude when it was neglected. It was still possible for a bishop to preside at the baptism of an infant, perform the anointing at that time, and administer communion to the child immediately. In England, this was done for royalty as late as the time of the birth of Henry VIII's children, Elizabeth (1533) and Edward (1537). But for the most part, the regulation effected the excommunication of children, even though this was far from being its purpose.

Elsewhere, the excommunication of children was achieved by a different route. It had been the practice of priests to administer a bit of wine to infants by dipping a finger into the chalice and then placing the finger in the infant's mouth; but infants were not given the eucharistic bread, because it was feared they could not digest solid food or might choke on it. As the doctrine of transubstantiation took hold, the administration of wine became more and more of a practical problem in the communion of adults. The priest could readily prevent the desecration of the bread by placing it directly upon the tongue of the communicant while an assistant held a vessel under the chin, lest the priest accidentally drop the bread or the communicant eject it involuntarily. But there was the danger that in administering the chalice some of the wine would be spilled, or that it would drip down the chin, or remain in a  mustache or beard. Therefore, it was deemed wise to have the wine received only by the celebrating priest. Theologically the reception of the bread only could be justified by the doctrine of concomitance: the full body and blood of Christ are present in each eucharistic element.

Here again we see the phenomenon of a practice's beginning for one set of reasons and being perpetuated for quite another set of reasons. What was intended as a practice in the case of adults (who could receive the bread) came to be applied also to infants, even though the danger of desecration was negligible, for the priest administered wine to them from his finger rather than from the chalice directly. Because infants were not given the bread for practical reasons, the withdrawal of the wine from them resulted in their excommunication. The Eucharist was inaccessible to them, if not until confirmation, at least until they could eat bread—and ultimately until they could make their first conscious act of penance. For penance also had come to be regarded as a sacrament, and apart from it communion was not to be given. (While ideally confirmation preceded the initial act of penance and communion, in practice penance and first communion often came to precede confirmation and to have a status superior to it, in the popular mind, at least.)

Thus, we see the total disintegration of the ancient baptismal practice of administering water, oil, and the Eucharist in a single liturgical celebration. By the end of the middle ages the original pattern of the church's initiation process is totally obscured, and the original understanding of the meaning of Christian initiation has been thoroughly revised. The effects of the developments across twelve centuries can be summarized in four categories.

(1) Baptism came to be viewed individualistically rather than corporately. Even when a congregation was present, the people were there primarily as observers. No longer did the clergy give voice to the whole people assembled and perform representative actions on behalf of the congregation. Instead, the clergy acted in lieu of the congregation.

(2) Baptism became mechanical and its effects were pinpointed in time. The ambiguity and dynamic expansiveness of the sacrament that characterized the early understanding of worship and of grace disappeared. Theologians identified the precise moment in the liturgy at which the sacramental action took effect. Instead of being a process, baptism came to be identified with the moment at which the water was administered. The work of the Holy Spirit, rather than seen as pervading the whole process, was understood to be associated with particular actions, especially with the action of the bishop in confirmation.

(3) The rite became more legal than liturgical. The question as to whether or not a particular baptism could be regarded as valid became important; that validity could be determined on the basis of identifiable criteria: water applied with the words "In the name of the Father and of the Son and of the Holy Spirit," and with the intention of doing what the church does. Thus, one could pass upon whether or not a particular individual had been properly baptized. More important was the fact that a person must be so baptized in order to attain eternal life.

(4) Perhaps most disastrously, baptism came to be viewed as something primarily negative—the removal of original guilt. The positive aspect of being called to serve and of receiving grace to carry out one's ministry was associated with the later rite of confirmation. The richness of biblical imagery associated with baptism in the early centuries, while still found in liturgical formulations, was largely obscured, due both to the people's ignorance of Scripture and the inability of most worshipers to understand the Latin text of the rites.

This, then, was the situation that prevailed in the church on the eve of the Reformation.

## COMPLICATIONS AND CONFUSION FROM THE REFORMATION ONWARD

The reformers sensed that something was amiss, but they did not have direct access to the documents of the ancient church, and could not accurately assess how far things had gone wrong over the centuries. Even the information they did have was read through the lenses of medieval interpretation. Thus, for example, the reformers insisted that baptism be administered in the presence of the congregation, except in extreme necessity; but (as even this exception shows) they continued to tie sacramental baptism closely to a rigid doctrine of original sin, either by modifying the relationship between the two (rejecting the notion of limbo and purgatory as intermediate states between heaven and hell, as Luther and Calvin did) or by so over-reacting to the relationship as to refuse to call baptism a sacrament, making it instead merely an ordinance for mature believers (as the Anabaptists did).

Luther, in particular, did see the weakness in tying the effect of baptism to the moment of the administration of the water. He rightly insisted that baptism has a continuing effect in the life of the Christian, and is a source of such great strength that there is no greater comfort on earth than the affirmation, "I am baptized." Calvin injected dynamism into baptism by emphasizing its covenantal character, and by interpreting the baptism of infants corporately; unfortunately, in doing this, he relied heavily upon a correlation between circumcision and baptism, an association that is problematic at best. Zwingli, while he momentarily agreed with the Anabaptists that infants should not be baptized, basically supported the traditional practice, even while holding that baptism is only an ordinance, which presupposes a confession of faith; when infants are baptized, he argued, it is in virtue of the faith of the whole congregation to which they belong.

While the radical wing of the reformation renounced the baptism of infants, and insisted that all who had undergone rites in infancy were not truly baptized, their concern had to do with the age of the candidates more than with the mode by which the water had been administered. Unlike later Baptists (who would share their views concerning the baptism of mature believers only), the Anabaptists commonly baptized by pouring, not by immersion.[5]

All the reformers saw the need for adult commitment and the propriety of its liturgical expression, but they came at this in different ways. All objected to the notion that, without confirmation, baptism is somehow incomplete or inadequate; and they rejected much of the ceremonial of the confirmation rite, particularly the use of oil (which they sometimes referred to derisively as grease) as tending toward superstition. Luther devised a form of catechetical instruction for young people, upon the completion of which they were admitted to first communion. While he himself did not include the laying on of hands, later Lutherans did; but even in the places that had bishops, Lutheran confirmation was pastoral rather than episcopal. Calvin also required instruction and affirmation of faith for admission to the Lord's Table. He advocated the laying on of hands, interpreted as an act of blessing rather than as a sacramental imparting of the Holy Spirit or gifts of the Spirit; but he did not implement this practice in Geneva. The Church of England adopted episcopal imposition of hands after catechesis as being necessary for admission to the Eucharist, but without sacramental character or use of oil; there was, however, an emphasis upon the strengthening work of the Spirit in confirmation, which later gave rise to controversy over whether the "seal of the Spirit" is given in baptism or only later at confirmation.[4]

Thus, in one way or another, the reformers perpetuated the Lambeth decision of 1281 that baptized persons are not to be admitted to communion without confirmation. Here again we see a practice instituted for one reason being perpetuated for quite a different reason. Lambeth had no objection to communion at an early age, but merely wanted to insure that those baptized by a priest were also confirmed by a bishop. The reformers, in insisting upon catechetical instruction before communion, unwittingly opened the door to a more cognitive approach to the Eucharist. Their concern was that Christians must be informed in order to be committed disciples in adulthood; they were not intending to make the Lord's Supper a more cerebral experience, only to prevent it from being a superstitious or meaningless event. Calvin, for example, delighted in the unfathomable mystery of the Lord's presence in the Eucharist through the power of the Holy Spirit. In view of the widespread ignorance of the people in their time, the reformers said what had to be said about the education of the laity. But later their affirmation was taken to mean that the Eucharist itself is perceived primarily at a cognitive level; thus, participation in the Lord's Supper became a privilege for those who presumed to understand it, or else was rejected as pre-scientific nonsense by rationalists who discovered they could not understand it. In either case, the mystery of grace offered to the whole company of the baptized in the Eucharist was obscured.

The reformers' assessment of the baptismal practices they inherited was perceptive, if incomplete. But the reforms themselves often served only to complicate matters further and to lay the foundation for greater confusion. Problems inherent in the reformation position were magnified in later eras. The cleavage between baptism and confirmation became more pronounced. Lutherans developed intensive confirmation programs equal in length to the ancient catechumenate. The Puritan emphasis on public profession of faith by those who had been baptized into the covenant faith in infancy became so strong that the importance of the sacrament itself was greatly diminished. The rise of rationalism and of pietism in Europe resulted, respectively, in a rejection of sacraments as pre-scientific superstition and in a devaluation of the sacraments as distinctly inferior to inner, personal experience. In the nineteenth and twentieth centuries, particularly in America, the picture becomes still more complex due to revivalism and pentecostalism, on the one hand, and liberalism, on the other.

Revivalism placed great emphasis upon commitment; but unlike the reformers (apart from some Anabaptists), it stressed subjective experience more than catechesis. While this was something of a necessary corrective to post-reformation scholasticism, which had become picayune about fine points of doctrine, it both fed upon and fed a heady individualism and anti-intellectualism. Far from reinforcing the reformation ideal of an informed faith as the basis for a faithful life, revivalism frequently seemed to argue against such a uniting of knowledge and vital piety. The personal experience of the individual was the crucial mark of a Christian; "book larnin' " (about theology, at least) was secondary, and might even be detrimental to faith.[5] Baptism and confirmation, if not completely unrelated to conversion, were at least unimportant to it.

For Baptists, the administration of water could only follow the personal religious experience, and thus testify to it; there was little hint that the personal experience might grow out of and be facilitated by the grace proclaimed in baptism and the nurture of the baptized by the covenant community. For non-Baptists, the adult experience could follow baptism, but without any clear relationship between the two events. Indeed, conversion might not occur until well after some formal post-baptismal event (be it called confirmation, catechism class, or simply "joining the church"). Among some non-Baptists who did not have formal confirmation, joining the church was reserved for the consciously converted; but for other non-Baptists, the sequence was readily reversed. Indeed, not infrequently the newly converted loved to boast that they had been church members for years before becoming Christians—a claim symptomatic of those who reject an ecclesiology that stresses sacraments, corporateness, and catechesis.

Thus, in revivalist circles, the Augustinian definition of a sacrament as an outward and visible sign of an inward and spiritual grace came to be transmuted into the tacit assumption that a sacrament is an unimportant and sometimes utterly empty ceremony, far inferior to an inward and invisible subjective experience of grace.

Somewhat later, much of the same low view of the sacraments found a home in Pentecostalist circles. There, however, baptism was given a place one rung farther down the ladder. Baptism was subsidiary to conversion, but both were secondary to the reception of the gifts of the Spirit in a charismatic experience. Further, the phrase "baptism of the Spirit" was often used in deliberate contrast to, and with an implied disparagement of, baptism with water. Without knowing it (and they would have been shocked to discover it), Pentecostalists simply accepted a variation of the ultra-high theology of confirmation. In both instances, baptism is considered to be incomplete and requires some additional action by God in order to be effective; the gift of the Spirit, whether given through episcopal action in a formal rite or through an informal charismatic experience, is detached from baptism itself.

If the contemporary low regard Protestants have for baptism springs in part from a revivalistic and Pentecostalist heritage, it also has its basis partially in an unimaginative liberal reaction to rationalism. Under the guise of scientific objectivity, rationalists virtually finished the demolition of the sacraments, and theological liberals were thrown into confusion about the meaning of baptism in particular.

In the past century and a half, two mighty assaults have been launched against the doctrine of original sin—the doctrine that in one form or another was linked to baptism by those reformers who retained the rite as a sacrament. First, Charles Darwin told us that there were no historical first parents named Adam and Eve. That took care of "original." Then Sigmund Freud, with others, assured us that God is a projection of infantile dependency and that guilt is a neurotic manifestation. That took care of "sin." Those who wished to retain baptism as a sacrament (particularly one for infants), and yet wanted to be scientifically respectable, found themselves in a quagmire.

The liturgical evidence of this perplexity on the part of liberals is nowhere more evident than in the development of the baptismal rites in American Methodism during the twentieth century. The traditional Methodist service for the baptism of infants, borrowed from the Anglicans, began by saying, "Forasmuch as all men are conceived and born in sin. . . ." In 1910, the Methodist Episcopal Church, South, changed this to read, "Forasmuch as all men, though fallen in Adam, are born into this world in Christ the Redeemer, heirs of eternal life and subjects of the saving grace of the Holy Spirit. . . ." In 1916, the northern denomination, the Methodist Episcopal Church, equally uncomfortable with the old formulation, and apparently a bit less sure about the existence of Adam, revised the general address to read: "Forasmuch as God in his great mercy hath entered into covenant relation with man. . . ." By 1932, the northern body revised its rites again, this time offering two rites of baptism, introduced as follows:

LONGER RITE
 Forasmuch as all children are members of the kingdom of God and therefore graciously entitled to Baptism. . . .

SHORTER RITE
 Forasmuch as this child is now presented by you for Christian Baptism. . . .

One can hardly miss the shift within a quarter of a century from original guilt theology, to covenant theology with an implied universalism, to a rather explicit universalism, to an almost blatant humanism. By the final stage, it is exceedingly unclear in the entire rite (not merely in the general address) what God does in baptism, if anything. But it is rather evident that baptism has nothing to do with sin, inherited or actual.

Indeed the 1932 shorter rite for the baptism of infants in the northern church contains no mention of sin, nor even an allusion to it, except in the Lord's Prayer, where the term is conveniently disguised under the word "trespass."

While the American Methodists of the early twentieth century may have been more given to tinkering with their liturgies than were other denominations, they were by no means alone in their confusion and perplexity. In a number of Protestant denominations (including the Methodist) the baptism of infants came to be rejected by some people in favor of a service of "dedication of infants." This was not based on a well-thought-out view of baptism as the sacramental initiation rite for the mature, but simply upon an inability to find any defensible meaning in baptism as a sacrament. The streams of revivalism-pentecostalism and of liberalism converged with disastrous results.

By now we need not marvel that the view of baptism that existed in the first three or four centuries seems so alien to many Christians today. So great is a sixteen-hundred-year legacy of contradiction and confusion that we can hardly imagine the situation's being otherwise. And is it any wonder that Lucy was taken in turn to the Wesleyan chapel, the Church of England, and the Salvation Army Citadel, only to be baptized again at puberty, and then in adulthood to be required to submit to immersion? Perhaps what should amaze us is the fact that the practice of baptism has survived sufficiently intact to allow the Holy Spirit to give us new insight into it in our age, and to motivate us to reform its practice in the church today.

We, therefore, now face another question—not merely, "What went wrong?" but, "How can we set things right?"

# 7

# HOW CAN WE SET THINGS RIGHT?

A renaissance of baptismal theology and practice is not likely to occur by accident, but will emerge only with deliberate action. Those who work toward a new appreciation of the sacrament will need to give careful attention both to content and strategy; for good theology will not be accepted if it is poorly presented, nor can the best techniques of communication cover the weaknesses of inadequate content. Therefore, we turn now to these two concerns.

## CONTENT

The content that pertains to a renewed understanding of baptism has been the subject of the early chapters of this book and need not be repeated in detail. But major aspects of that content can be summarized here.

Crucial to the recovery of baptism is an emphasis upon the nature of God, particularly upon God as the covenant-maker. Both the divine initiative on our behalf and the divine imperative upon us are crucial facets of this emphasis. The Christian faith centers upon a God who acts graciously toward us, thus both calling forth and empowering our response.

Because God's most definitive activity is seen in Jesus Christ, the content we speak about must also deal with Christology. The baptized are not merely those who are trying to become like Jesus; they are those who are saved by and incorporated into Jesus Christ. We cannot know what it is to be "in Christ" until we have wrestled with the question, "Who is this Jesus whom we call the Christ of God?" And this leads us to an appreciation of the cosmic Christ who recapitulates all that has been, and anticipates and brings into being all that will be.

A sacramental theology that springs from the conviction that God acts through the cosmic Christ will bring us to the theology of creation and consummation. This bears directly upon the very existence of sacramental experience. For unless the world is God's handiwork, the notion that God communicates through water will be incomprehensible, or even repugnant; and unless creation is moving toward the fulfillment of God's purpose, there is no future toward which the sacraments can point; the divine promises they signify are empty. Furthermore, a view of God's purposeful activity from creation to consummation gives us a view of the sacraments that is dynamic and expansive, rather than mechanical and tied to particular isolated moments (especially to the moment at which the water is administered). Baptism is from the past, linking us to all God has already done; and baptism is for the present and the future, continually shaping our lives as we already participate in, and yet await, the coming kingdom.

The concept of the kingdom that already is and yet is still to be draws our attention to the need for a renewed ecclesiology. Baptism is intimately tied to the doctrine of the church, and therefore reflects what our ecclesiology tells us about the relationship of individuals in the community of faith and the relationship of that community of the world. The renewal of baptismal theology will be related to our ability to counter a strong individualism, which atomizes the church by viewing it as a voluntary collection of individuals with similar beliefs, rather than as the organic body of Christ set within the world as a harbinger of the wholeness and righteousness God wills for that world. Furthermore, it must be plainly seen that Christian identity is not something persons find individually outside of the church and then bring to it, but instead is something that is discovered within the community and carried forth to be shared.

All of this points to the need for a more solid theology of the work of the Holy Spirit. Too often we are silent about pneumatology unless we are confronted with a position we feel compelled to refute. Thus our doctrine of the Spirit is perceived as being vague, or defensive, or both. There can be little hope for the renewal of baptism in the church until we recover the conviction that the sacraments are the gifts of the Spirit of the Risen Lord within the church, and that the Spirit works both through objective acts and through the subjective appropriation of those acts. Without the objective fact that God constitutes the covenant and gives us an indelible identity through baptism, our subjective experience of God easily slips over into mere sentimentality. Without the subjective reality of our experience of, and response to, God's grace, objectivity can produce a sacramentalism that is remote from life and falls prey to mechanistic or even superstitious interpretation. It is in a sound doctrine of the Holy Spirit that we find the way to maintain the critical balance between the objective and the subjective.

The content needed for the proper recovery of baptism is nothing short of the full scope of Christian theology; or, to put it in picturesque form: those who take hold of the little finger known as liturgy quickly discover that they have grabbed the whole fist of theology.[1] What is before us, then, is nothing less than the work of total theological renewal in our time. It is apparent that the task must be deliberately assumed and carefully planned.

While the very existence of sacramental actions and things is testimony that words are not everything in communicating the faith, this by no means indicates that words are unimportant. Either the nonverbal and the verbal will complement each other, or they will be in conflict with each other. In teaching, preaching, and writing about the sacraments, we need to watch our language carefully. If theologians appear to be semantic hair-splitters, it is because hard experience has taught us what tragic results can occur when language is used casually or imprecisely. Therefore, some very concrete suggestions about language are in order.

Great care should be taken with respect to the subjects of sentences, the verbs selected, and the use of prepositions when setting forth sacramental theology. For example, here are three related statements that at first may seem harmless, but that harbor potential for misunderstanding and distortion:

1. The sacraments convey [transmit, channel, confer] grace.
2. At your baptism you received God's gift.
3. Therefore baptism saves you.

The first sentence, employing any of the four verbs, represents a rather classic formulation; yet such wording has resulted in much misunderstanding.[2] Certainly the sacraments are related to grace, as opposed to being empty forms that have no effect. But any of the verbs indicated tends toward a mechanical interpretation, as if baptism were a conveyor belt for grace, and as if grace were a commodity that could be neatly packaged and delivered. Furthermore, the subject of the sentence places the focus upon the instrument rather than upon the One who chooses to use that instrument.

The second sentence suffers similar weaknesses. The preposition "at" may imply that whatever happens sacramentally is tied to the moment of administration, period. The verb used in the past tense reinforces this, and in addition, injects again the mechanical implication, as though the gift were thrust upon a passive recipient from whom nothing is expected.

The third statement is particularly problematic because it is utterly biblical; at least the RSV translates I Peter 3:21 in exactly this way. But in the context here (which is different from that of the Epistle), the subject and verb are troublesome; they reinforce the weaknesses of the first two sentences. Thus, all three statements have a potential for generating confusion, and even sacramental heresy.

Now let us rephrase the sentences in a way that makes their meaning more theologically adequate and less open to misinterpretation:

1. God acts graciously in the sacraments.
2. Through your baptism you receive God's gifts.
3. Thus you are baptized into Christ for the forgiveness of sin.

In the reconstructed first sentence, God is the subject; thus baptism is seen as a means of divine revelation, not as an end in itself. The verb "acts" is more open than any of the verbs previously used. The use of the adverb "graciously" rather

136

than the noun "grace" connects God's goodness with dynamic activity, rather than with the static image of a commodity. "In" is a relatively open preposition that does not seem to restrict God's activity and freedom. ("Through" is an even better preposition for this purpose, but it is used at the beginning of the next sentence, and variety has its virtue in communication.)

The revised second sentence does not imply that the benefits of baptism are restricted to a particular moment. "Through" and "receive" help to indicate that baptism, while administered only once to each individual, is a perpetual sacrament through which God can speak to us again and again. Putting "gift" in plural form reinforces this expansive understanding of God's work.

The third statement has been altered in a way that connects baptism with forgiveness, but does not suggest that the sacrament itself produces salvation in an automatic way. The revision makes more evident the theological understanding that God through baptism incorporates us into Christ's atoning and justifying work. Salvation is found in Christ, to whom we are bound in baptism, rather than in the rite itself.

The careful use of language also involves avoiding weak words that say less than we mean. In revising the second sentence, for example, it is tempting to say, "Through baptism you are offered God's gifts." This would certainly help to eliminate the notion of automatic transmittal of grace, for an offer means little until it has been accepted. Yet, for precisely this reason, "offer" says too little about baptism. A covenant is more than an offer. It is an action requiring a response; it is a promise that actually affects us and gives us an indelible identity, even though we may react to it with indifference or rebelliousness rather than with faithful obedience. Furthermore, baptism initiates us into a community of faith that assumes a responsibility for the future of those who are baptized without waiting for them to ask for concern and help. Thus, to suggest merely that through baptism God offers us something, is to settle for a devastatingly weak theology.

The three sentences discussed here are not intended to set forth a comprehensive theology of baptism; yet they do illustrate how much meaning is packed into a few words, and with what care we need to choose those words if we are to communicate adequately what we believe.

Another matter of concern when referring to the sacraments has to do with the choice between the word *symbol* and the word *sign*. The distinction between these terms is a complex one because of the way the connotations of the words have changed. Originally *symbol* was a powerful term. Etymologically it is derived from a Greek phrase that means "to bring together"—literally, to throw together with force. Understood in this way, a sacramental symbol is the fusion of the material element and the reality that element communicates; that is, the vehicle is utterly bound to the truth it carries.

In much popular discourse today, however, *symbol* is a weak term that has a disparaging connotation. Thus, we can dismiss the importance of a gesture by saying, "Well, after all, it is only a symbol." The implication is that the gesture may, or may not, represent reality. Therefore, if we speak of sacraments as symbols, our hearers may take us to mean that baptism and the Eucharist are merely vague reminders of divine grace, and that the reality of God's goodness is detached from these. Then the sacraments are readily dismissed as being "*just* symbols." (It should be noted in passing that Paul Tillich sought to reclaim the original force of the term *symbol* and to give it superiority over *sign*. In principle, he was correct in his attempt; in practice, however, he probably inaugurated a futile battle against the prevailing mood.)

In our society, the term *sign* communicates more adequately what we want to say about sacraments. *Sign* has a long and technical theological history (as does the related term *significance*). This is both bane and blessing—bane because we can get tangled in the technicalities, but blessing because we can draw upon the positive aspects of our heritage, including the importance of signs in Scripture. What concerns us primarily here, however, is the connotations words have at the popular level today.

Some rather pedestrian examples may clarify the contemporary connotation of *sign*. When an artist draws some red marks to indicate flames and a black spiral to indicate smoke, we think of these as being symbols of fire. We do not call the fire department because the symbols are not directly attached to the reality; they merely remind us of it. But when we observe flames and billows of smoke issuing forth from a building, we take that to be more than a symbol of fire. It is a sign that something is actually burning, and we rush for the nearest telephone. Or to use another example: Wedding bands on display in a jewelry store window are symbols of marriage; they remind us in a nonspecific way that matrimony exists. But a wedding band on someone's hand is more than a symbol of marriage; assuming that no deception is intended, the band is a reliable sign that the wearer is married.

There is another dimension to the nuances of the words *symbol* and *sign*. Because *symbol* is regarded as the weaker designation, it can be useful for putting into perspective secondary sacramental objects or actions; we can then reserve *sign* for the central activity of the sacrament. Thus in baptism the water and its application constitute the sign to which the promise of God is attached. If we also use a baptismal candle, new clothes, or a chalice of milk and honey, these are symbols that point toward what is signified in the washing with water. Valuable as the auxiliary rites may be, they are not of the essence. These symbols complement the sign, but can never be substitutes for it.

Another homely experience may help to clarify the nuances here. Suppose you are driving on an interstate highway with an almost empty gas tank. Above the trees you see a logo that is symbolic of a petroleum company. This symbol indicates that there is a service station nearby. Yet, helpful though that may be, the symbol tells you nothing about whether the station is closed, open for repairs only, or open to sell gasoline. What is of primary concern to you is the "pumps open" sign you hope to see once you have driven off the exit ramp. The symbol complements the sign, and even directs you to it; but apart from that sign, the symbol is bare and may even mock you. The baptismal candle, the new clothes, the milk and honey do symbolize what baptism signifies: enlightenment, the newness of life we put on in Christ, entrance into the promise. Yet only the sign enables the symbols to work effectively.

A deliberate choice between *symbol* and *sign* can be crucial if we are to present the kind of theology needed for the recovery of baptism in our time. In preaching, teaching, and more informal pastoral discussion, it often may not be advisable to go into a discourse on the difference between the two terms. Calling attention to what may be perceived by many as a minor and even incomprehensible distinction can indeed cause a still greater devaluation of sacramental theology. Yet simply being aware of the differences in connotation, and avoiding the less appropriate term, will go a long way toward enabling Christians to appreciate fully the sacrament of their initiation into Jesus Christ.

This discussion of language touches only a minute part of our concern for careful expression, and is intended to produce awareness of the kinds of problems that exist, without identifying or elaborating upon every possible difficulty. Furthermore, a distinction should be made about the care we take in prepared statements and the less precise use of language characteristic of more casual settings. In conversation and extemporaneous presentations, precision in content is difficult; certainly a concern for careful expression should not terrify us of talking about baptism without a prepared manuscript. Yet when there is opportunity for preparation in writing (whether sermon, articles for a parish newsletter, statements of policy, or prayers used at the time of baptism) our use of words should be scrutinized. Over a period of time, careful attention to statements that are formulated in advance will increase our precision, even in off-the-cuff remarks.

## STRATEGY

The recovery of sound baptismal theology and practice requires attention to method as well as to content. Too much material introduced to a congregation too quickly can produce theological or liturgical indigestion. Particularly in parishes where little thought has been given to baptism for generations, a sudden concerted effort may convey the impression that we are simply pushing the latest fad, or that we are making mountains out of the proverbial molehills. On the other hand, timidity can seem to indicate that baptism really isn't that important after all. If an appropriate balance is to be struck, an appraisal of each situation will be required if those responsible for worship are to know how to proceed effectively.

In general, however, an approach that is extended over several years is the most likely to allow for assimilation, and to provide an opportunity for periodic evaluations and necessary adjustments in course. In planning and carrying out such a program of sacramental renewal, several areas require specific attention. Because baptism is a liturgical act, obviously the service of worship itself comes to mind as the place to begin. However, this matter is sufficiently important to be the concern of a separate chapter. Here we shall make some statements about a general educational approach toward baptism, and about programs related to the affirmation of baptism and pre-baptismal instruction; in connection with the latter area, it is necessary to broach the delicate subject of deferring and refusing baptism. Then we shall turn to matters of parish policy related to baptism, and of introducing and evaluating change within a congregation. Finally, the matter of ministerial courtesy will be discussed.

Educational efforts at all age levels should be given careful attention. An adult study course can be offered on baptism, or on sacraments more generally. It is advisable to schedule this at some time other than the Sunday church school hour; for the church school teachers should themselves be able to attend, in order that they may in turn incorporate a basic understanding of baptism in their teaching.

The curriculum materials of the church school may need evaluation and revision at key points. Because the approach to baptism I have been taking has come into focus quite recently, it has not yet been assimilated into church publications, for the most part. Indeed, such publications may perpetuate misunderstandings of baptism (particularly as confirmation is related to it), or may say almost nothing at all about Christian initiation. Ultimately, denominational and inter-denominational curriculum committees will take such matters into account when materials are revised according to systematic scheduling. During the interim, however, local churches may need to analyze the materials and seek supplementary resources as required.

Instead of carrying out this task separately, it can be more effective for parishes using the same or closely related curriculum materials to do joint evaluations, and to consider revisions that are useful to all involved. In fact, as new materials prepared and used in such co-operative ventures are tested in a variety of situations and are further modified, the results can be useful to denominational and cooperative curriculum planning groups.

Where possible, study experiences themselves should be jointly conducted by several parishes, with as much ecumenical breadth as is possible in the local situation. Not only will this facilitate dialogue and understanding among various groups; of more importance is the fact that such an approach grows out of, and incarnates, the unity God has given to us in baptism.[5]

Particular educational attention will need to be given to programs designed for those who were baptized in infancy or childhood and who later make a public affirmation of the baptismal covenant. In the past, such a time of affirmation has often been viewed as a point of arrival rather than as a way-station; baptized children progressed through the various levels of the church school, and finally completed the course at about the time of puberty. Churches that have placed a heavy emphasis upon a concentrated program at the end of the period have found that too often such an effort (commonly called "confirmation class") is regarded as a form of graduation from the process of Christian education—or even from the active life of the church. Among those for whom such a program was prerequisite for admission to the Lord's Table, there arose a bitter piece of humor that refers to this admission as "last communion," rather than "first communion."

Because the renewal of baptism is a lifelong process, which for those who were baptized at an early age begins consciously at puberty or thereafter, the perception and programs related to renewal require change. The initial act of public renewal has to be seen as the beginning of a conscious life of ministry that characterizes all committed Christians. Educational materials and approaches used at the time of the affirmation of the covenant need to be clearly related, both to the covenant promise already given by God, and to the covenantal loyalty that is to be maintained by us until death.

The importance of the first public renewal of the

baptismal covenant and its relationship to the obedient life of service raises the issue of the appropriate age for first affirmation. Influenced perhaps by the story of Jesus in the temple at the age of twelve, and reinforced by contemporary *bar mitzvah* and *bat mitzvah* practices in Judaism, parishes have tended to suggest that affirmation should occur at the sixth or seventh grade level; undoubtedly the choice of this age has also resulted from a reluctance to bar people older than twelve or thirteen from the Lord's Table. Dissatisfaction with this pattern has been occasioned both by the graduation mentality, and by the realization that the complexities of our world and the variety of possible responses to these tangled problems by mature Christians may better be addressed during the years of senior high school, when students are more aware of the social order. Those who favor the usual age note that our youth seem to mature earlier and earlier, particularly as educational approaches in our schools increasingly deal with sophisticated subjects at lower grade levels; they add that, while twelve and thirteen-year-old people may not be terribly aware of the complexities of disarmament or global hunger in relation to Christian action, they are already confronted with the drug culture and with the possibilities of pregnancy and abortion— matters that also require Christian analysis and response.

A possible practical way around this impasse involves a more flexible approach to affirmation of the covenant and preparation for adult discipleship. For example, the usual pastor's class can be divided into segments of pre-affirmation and post-affirmation study. Post-affirmation study may follow the act of covenant renewal by some distance when a rite at the age of twelve or thirteen is expedient. While moving toward renewal at a later age seems preferable, in some circumstances it is not advisable due to the tug of custom or force of peer pressure from schoolmates in other congregations that do have an affirmation rite at the earlier age.

Particularly when affirmation is likely to occur early, we should take care to say to those who enter into a pre-affirmation program, "At the end of our time together some of you may feel that you are ready to make your first public affirmation of the baptismal covenant. There will be opportunity for you to do that at the Easter Vigil [or other designated time]. But there will be other similar opportunities for public renewal further in the future; many of you may well decide to wait awhile before taking this important step." If we can encourage participation of the baptized in the Lord's Supper from an early age, and if we can free ourselves from that slavery to statistical measurements of church growth that drives us to admit to adult-membership-status people of a set age each year, then we can develop a more healthy atmosphere in which youth truly consider the implications of the baptismal covenant without pressure to conform within a certain period of time.

Thus far, we have avoided calling the affirmation process *confirmation*. There are several reasons. A good case can be made for equating the term *confirmation* with the act of chrismation at baptism; in the previous chapter we noted the confusion that resulted from the separation of these two aspects of the ancient baptismal liturgy. But because Protestants, in particular, have so closely linked what we call confirmation with the process of education for adult discipleship, the restoration of baptism-confirmation as a single rite can be misunderstood to mean that later conscious commitment by those baptized in infancy is no longer required or expected. This certainly is not the case; therefore, it is desirable that the later process be given a designation (such as "affirmation of the baptismal covenant") that clarifies its relation to the sacrament.

It is only realistic, however, to recognize that in some denominations and congregations the term *confirmation* will continue to be used for the renewal process. Then care should be taken to give a broader definition than has generally existed. Confirmation is to be understood as more than a series of catechism classes, but as less than an independent sacrament that "completes," or even overshadows, baptism. Further, confirmation is more than a religious way of recognizing the cultural reality attached to puberty, but less than a mandatory rite of passage into Christian maturity at a specific age level.

Regardless of the name it goes under, the first public renewal of baptism does not deserve the status that has frequently been conferred upon confirmation at puberty. What is crucial for the Christian life is that there be an ongoing renewal and commitment, a taking up of the cross daily.

Periodic liturgical acts of renewal remind us of this and motivate us to follow in the way of the Lord. A specific liturgical act of first public affirmation by those baptized in infancy can be a helpful step in the process. But it is a means, not an end. The possibility that conscientious youth may defer or even entirely skip affirmation during adolescence because they feel they are not ready to make such a commitment is a risk preferable to the possibility that some youth, moved more by social pressure than by understanding and conviction, go through the motions, and then drop out of church life. The potential for mature commitment during adulthood may be greater in the former instance than in the latter.

While denominational polity may sometimes distort matters ("You can't have your name on the full membership roll until you have been formally confirmed"), or while in some cases liturgical action by a bishop is deemed necessary, the public act of renewal by individuals at a set time is not the sacred cow it has been made to seem. If the later act, whatever we call it, is not necessary to complete baptism, and if it is not necessary for admission to the Lord's Table, then this act can become what it ought to be: a useful way of making baptized people conscious of God's gracious gift and of their own intentional participation in the Christian covenant.

Until recently, denominations that had rites of both baptism and confirmation commonly required the latter even for those who were baptized as adults. Parishes accustomed to this practice will need to be helped to realize that unless the laying on of hands by a bishop is required and the bishop has not participated in baptism, those baptized as adults are not to be confirmed. An act of renewal imposed on an act of conscious entrance into the covenant is redundant at best, and a trifle insulting at worst (as when people are asked almost immediately after the water has been administered, "Do you renew the solemn promise and vow that you made at your baptism?").

Sacramental renewal in the parish will include careful attention to the preparation of candidates for baptism and, in the case of infants, of their parents or other sponsors. Pastors of small congregations may wish to approach such instruction on a case-by-case basis. In larger parishes, group sessions may be held. In any situation, however, co-operative programs should be explored. When churches of more than one denomination can plan and conduct such sessions together, this will help illustrate the meaning of baptism. Even the usual inclination to have joint study on the basic theological issues and then to divide into separate groups to discuss denominational history and polity may be challenged to the benefit of all. Members of one denomination can learn much about their own heritage as it parallels or contrasts with that of other denominations. Why should Methodists not learn what a presbytery is, for example, or how congregational polity differs from connectional polity? Where rigid approaches and animosities can be put aside, it is possible for groups as diverse as Roman Catholic, Baptist, and United Church of Christ to participate in joint pre-baptismal endeavors.

The form and content of pre-baptismal training will vary according to local needs and will depend upon whether the group consists of the parents of infants, mature candidates, or both. In either case, however, careful attention to biblical and theological matters should be given primary emphasis. The material in the early chapters of this book can be adapted for study and discusson in a pre-baptismal program.

Failure of candidates or their parents to participate in pre-baptismal instruction is sufficient reason for the deferral, or even the refusal, of baptism. This brings us to one of the prickliest issues we shall consider: by what right and under what circumstances do we deny the sacrament of baptism?

In the vocabulary of the typical congregation (and usually in that of its pastor), the phrase *refusal of baptism* cannot be conceived to exist. We are told on every hand that God's people are to be accepting, affirming, and supportive of all sorts and conditions of humanity. Pastors who decline to perform some baptisms will be regarded as oddities by other clergy; and unless they make their reasons clear, they may find themselves in severe difficulty with their congregations. Nevertheless, long before now it must have been clear that, from the perspective of the theology of baptism discussed in this book, such refusals are not mere possibilities, but are necessities in certain instances—not only for the sake of the integrity of the sacrament and of the church, but also for the sake of those who request baptism without serious intention or understanding.

The arguments we commonly use to defend indiscriminate baptism need to be turned on their heads. Instead of saying, "Suppose we turn people off to the church by saying, 'No' " we would do well to ask, "Is there a chance that we may turn people on to the church by demanding something of them?" We have misjudged human nature in assuming that people are interested primarily in organizations that expect nothing. In fact, the most demanding groups tend to have the longest waiting lists. Or, to turn the coin over: all too often people simply settle down to the level of the low expectation we have of them, or rise to the challenge of the high expectations we hold.

The more sensitive side of the refusal of baptism emerges when the candidates are infants. Then we ask, "How can we refuse baptism to a helpless baby who surely should not be deprived of this sign of God's love simply because the parents have no real commitment to Christ?" But that question also needs to be turned around: "How can we allow helpless children to grow up with almost no chance of knowing what their baptism really means and ought to call forth from them, so that they come to regard their baptism as having been of no importance?" In a slightly different set of circumstances we may need to ask, "Given the fact that the parents come only with serious misunderstandings about baptism, can we visit upon defenseless children the illusion that baptism was a mechanical act that saved them from whatever horrors their parents supposed might await the unbaptized when they die?" Unless we view baptism as an almost magical act necessary for the salvation of the individual, it is difficult to defend indiscriminate baptism.

The instincts we like to call "pastoral" are not entirely wrong, to be sure; but when confronted with candidates or parents who seem to have no serious intent, we need to distinguish between the desire to be pastoral and the fear of being anything other than a pushover. When it is necessary to say, "no," or "wait," the reply should be given with the full graciousness that characterizes the gospel. The pastor makes a good start if the proper answers are given at the time of initial contact with candidates or parents. Instead of responding to a request for baptism with too positive an answer (from which it is then almost impossible to back away), or with an immediate refusal, it is better to proceed somewhat like this: "I am happy to learn of your interest in baptism, and will be glad to explore this possibility with you. Our church does have certain clear expectations of those who receive baptism, and I am sure you will want to know what these are. Also, we have opportunities for pre-baptismal discussion and training. Let's arrange a time when we can talk about these matters." This approach will also buy time when a pastor does not know the inquirer, and may be able to gain some insight into the situation from members of the congregation who do know the background of the request.

Even refusals can be stated in a way that leaves the door ajar: "In light of the expectations our church has of baptismal candidates, we feel that you need to consider further the step you propose to take and the responsibilities you would assume at baptism. Please give this careful thought over a period of time. Then perhaps you will want to come back and talk about baptism further. I hope so." Nor need the responsibility for refusal rest entirely upon the pastor. Congregations may consider adopting a practice that already exists in some denominations; candidates are interviewed and voted upon by a committee of the laity as well as by the clergy. Baptism is, after all, admission to the laity; and the practice of voting upon candidates is a very ancient and honorable one.

Ultimately, however, we must confront a basic reality—that neither individually as clergy, nor in committee with the laity, are we God. Therefore we will make errors of judgment. We can count on it. For example, experience tells us that often young people who have wandered away from the faith suddenly are grasped by a keen sense of spiritual responsibility when they become parents. Thinking we see in a particular couple that faint glimmer of renewed commitment, we decide to err, if at all, on the side of leniency. The beaming parents assume the vows of their first-born so convincingly—and disappear without a trace. What then? Worse yet, several years later they reappear out of nowhere, expecting that their second child will be baptized without question. Or, what if someone really *is* turned off to the Christian faith by a firm baptismal discipline?

In such situations there are no comfortable solutions easily arrived at. When it is apparent that a wrong judgment was made and that damage has resulted, then we who suffer accusing consciences may benefit most by recalling the meaning of our own baptism. We are yet in the land between the river of Eden and the river of the New Jerusalem; though going on to perfection, we are sinners still. We entrust our imperfections and errors to a gracious God, and move ahead as those who are saved by grace, not by our own attainment or wisdom. Nor should we allow our accusing consciences to convince us that we necessarily do more damage because of our imperfect powers of judgment than we would do by refusing to make any judgments at all, thereby devaluing the sacrament through its indiscriminate administration.

Baptismal education and discipline can be facilitated by written statements that outline the meaning of baptism and the procedures related to its celebration. In addition to stating theological formulations in language that is accessible to all, such statements should set forth the expectation, for example, that baptism is to occur as a part of the service of public worship, that candidates are to engage in a period of instruction, and that, in the case of infants, at least one of the parents shall be an active member of the parish. These documents can be given to those who inquire about baptism for their study between the time they make the request and the occasion of the first pre-baptismal discussion.

It is desirable that such statements be formulated by the congregational committee charged with responsibility for worship, be approved by the administrative body of the parish, and be distributed to all members. The writing and approving of such publications will in itself be an educative process in the parish. The more broadly based such statements can be, the less chances there are of misunderstanding when a neighbor's child is not granted immediate baptism, or when the niece of a trustee is told that her baptism is to take place during the Sunday service, not in her own home on a Thursday evening.

Those who introduce new policies and practices should heed the admonition of Jesus to be as wise as serpents and as harmless as doves, lest they end up being as hurtful as serpents and as defenseless as doves under gunfire. Care is needed in deciding what to introduce, when to present it, and how to evaluate it after a period of trial use.

It is probably safe to assume that in most congregations changes will be proposed first by the pastor, or at least at the pastor's suggestion. While initiative by the laity is commendable and is to be encouraged, we face the reality that laypersons are particularly reticent to step over onto what they consider to be the pastor's basic turf—the ordering of worship. Thus a primary consideration in introducing change has to do with pastoral authority and integrity.

Congregations that are light years away from the sacramental understanding of the person who has just become their pastor cannot be expected to embrace a host of new ideas within the first six weeks, or even six months—particularly if the new pastor has had little previous experience, and is apt to be dismissed as being "fresh out of school with unsound and untested ideas." The way to reform needs to be paved with an establishment of rapport and trust between pastor and people. Unfortunately, circumstances do not always respect this fact, and a new pastor whose ordination certificate is barely dry is up against it when the staunchest financial supporter of the parish demands to be rebaptized, "this time just like Jesus was." Such a situation will require the wisdom of a Solomon.

But the pastor who has been in the same congregation for ten years may not have an easy time of it either, though well established and respected. The task will be particularly difficult if it involves reversing previous policies and practices. How do pastors who have indiscriminately baptized all comers on any day of the week, and in private, suddenly convince the congregation that baptism is an act of corporate worship intended only for those who are committed and their children, provided they have not been baptized before? These pastors will need to share with their congregations the process by which they came to a change of conviction, and will need to deal patiently with the same attitudes toward baptismal discipline they themselves previously had.

Regardless of the length of a pastor's tenure, a plan with clear goals and realistic methods will be a valuable tool. What is the best way to begin? With a sermon on the meaning of baptism? With such a sermon in the context of a baptismal service that introduces some new practices? If so, how many innovations should be tried on the same Sunday? Perhaps the process should begin with a congregational study group, or with discussion and study in the worship committee. How quickly can a program proceed? Should a statement of congregational policy be worked out within the first six months of such a program, or is it better to wait a couple of years? Is this the time to suggest a plan of pre-baptismal education sponsored just by this congregation, or is the time ripe for doing this jointly with other parishes of the same denomination, or is it possible to work on this ecumenically?

No book should presume to answer such questions. Each local situation is different; pastors and others responsible for worship must evaluate a particular parish from within. Several generalizations can be made, however, about methods of introduction and evaluation.

Usually congregations (and human beings more generally, for that matter) resist what they do not understand. While liturgy is not something that should be explained to death before it is experienced, any word of introduction that can interpret a change without belaboring it probably will insure a more positive reaction than would otherwise result. If a congregation is not accustomed to baptisms in the context of the Sunday service, for example, a rationale for this drastic innovation will be in order before proceeding. This may take the form of a sermon on baptism in relation to the corporate character of the church, or of an article in the parish newsletter, or of a pastoral comment just before the service begins, or some combination of these procedures.

It is also helpful to note that the introduction of a new practice is not something the congregation will be stuck with permanently with no hope of recourse. At the same time, however, our penchant for being democratic sometimes drives us to try something for too short a period before assessing it. Habits are neither easily broken nor easily formed; hence to evaluate, after only two to three uses, an innovation that has displaced a long-standing custom is virtually to guarantee the rejection of that which is new. It is wiser to err on the side of a trial period that is a trifle too long than on the side of premature evaluation.

Another consideration has to do with the means by which we elicit congregational evaluation. Often we succumb to the written opinion poll approach. A questionnaire is included in the Sunday bulletin or the parish newsletter with the invitation to all to return it completed, but unsigned. Such an approach may partake of the harmlessness of doves, but hardly of the wisdom attributed to serpents. For usually those who are content with the changes do not bother to fill out the questionnaire. Thus, the returns represent a disproportionate amount of dissatisfaction. Even if the form requests demographic information, unless it is signed, it is impossible to know who is grinding which axes.

A preferable method of evaluation is this. Let the members of the worship committee or administrative body approach a sampling of active members whose opinions generally are respected, and who are in touch with the thinking of the rest of the congregation. Without trying to construct a scientifically balanced sample, attempts should be made to include in such a group people of various ages, theological persuasions, minority groups, and both sexes. Invite these people to attend a discussion meeting three or four weeks hence to talk about how they themselves respond to the changes, and what they perceive the responses of others to be. During the period between the invitation and the meeting, they can actively solicit the opinions of others. Members of the congregation may be urged to direct responses to these people, or the meeting may even be an open forum. Usually those who react irresponsibly to changes on the basis of emotion rather than substance are less inclined to air their biases at an open meeting than on an anonymous document. More important is the fact that in a discussion attitudes and reactions can be probed in a way that is impossible using the written opinion approach. At such an evaluation meeting, the members of the worship committee who planned the changes should interject as few of their own assessments as possible. Using what they hear, they can later make necessary modifications or compromises in order to achieve more effective liturgical practice.

One further matter of importance has to do with ministerial courtesy. Pastors who have patiently and skillfully introduced changes in their congregations have the right to expect that when they retire or move to another position those who follow them will continue the policies and practices to which those congregations are committed. The new pastor should fully understand the policies and practices before seeking to revise them. Arbitrary changes confuse and irritate parishioners, and betray a lack of respect for clergy colleagues.

Not only should new pastors seek to understand and to continue what their predecessors labored hard to achieve; incumbent pastors should respect the principles of clergy in other parishes, whether of their own denomination, or of another. Before admitting to candidacy someone who requests baptism, it is advisable to inquire, "Have you previously requested this sacrament of any other Christian pastor?" If an affirmative answer is given, the circumstances of the situation should be investigated before proceeding. The prospective candidate can be told, "I want to understand and respect the position of other pastors. Therefore, before I consider your request further, I wish to contact the pastor who denied you baptism. That pastor and I may, or may not, agree; but if I do decide to baptize you, at least I have respected the position of the other pastor sufficiently to discuss the matter and to disagree in an open manner."

Congregations will not come to see baptism as having central importance to the faith and unity of the church so long as new pastors arbitrarily overturn established reforms, and so long as someone can be denied the sacrament of baptism by a conscientious pastor in one parish, only to be received without question in another parish. Respect and consultation can help eliminate confusion on the part of the laity and feelings of bitterness and distrust among the clergy.

As should be clear by now, if we are to set things right we will need to pursue a multifaceted strategy. Periodic reviews of each facet will be helpful in evaluating progress toward the intended goals. The patient and deliberate attainment of such goals can help to renew the life of a congregation of Christ's covenant people.

# 8

# REFORM OF THE
# SERVICE OF BAPTISM

The service of baptism is itself the most conspicuous place at which to set forth the meaning of the sacrament. If the liturgy does not reflect the faith of the church, all other attempts to set things right will be diminished in their effectiveness, if not entirely cancelled. Hence this study concludes with observations about the baptismal rites and how we carry them out.

## WHAT PRACTICES TO RESTORE?

We may well wonder to what extent we should seek to revive ancient practices revealed in our study of early Christian patterns of baptismal liturgy. We must begin by observing that our task is not restoration for its own sake. Christian discipleship is not an archeological dig, and the church is not a museum for assorted liturgical artifacts. A crucial question to ask when contemplating the restoration of an ancient practice is, "What sense does it make in our age?"

Some things that have been largely abandoned make less sense in our time than do others. For example, to ask candidates for baptism to face west and to spit by way of renouncing the devil is a silly enterprise in twentieth-century America. In a society that depends heavily upon artificial illumination, east and west no longer convey the opposition of light and darkness they once did; and if evil is personified at all, chances are that such personification has more to do with a misguided satanism, or at least with a simplistic biblical literalism, than with any theological understanding we would wish to encourage. On the other hand, we do on occasion use lighted candles in our culture. Thus, to restore the presentation of the baptismal candle may seem quite natural, while turning to the west and spitting and then turning to the east would induce only discomfort or confusion.

Familiarity is not the only consideration, however. The use of oil in bathing is not a practice familiar to most of us. But while the abundant anointing that characterized the early rites may seem odd today, still, a judicious amount of oil applied to the forehead cannot be dismissed as an archaic gesture that should be ignored. For the name *Christ* means *anointed;* and our understanding of scriptural images both for Christ and for the Holy Spirit can be greatly enhanced by recovering chrismation, where congregational attitudes do not militate against it. Therefore, to the question of cultural familiarity must be added a more important question: will the restoration of an ancient practice open to our people meanings in the Bible that otherwise are hidden behind allusions the contemporary reader cannot recognize? If so, then it is worth at least exploring the possibility of reintroducing the ancient practice.

Often there are suggestions that instead of reproducing an early custom we should find its contemporary counterpart, and use that instead. Thus, someone may be tempted to ask, "If the ancients used oil with the ease that we use soap, why not use soap and a cloth to wash those receiving the sacrament?" The answer is that while we may have practices that are different, yet analogous, our customs may do nothing to open biblical imagery to us. The dove returning to the ark did not carry a bar of soap in its beak; the kings and priests of Israel were not scrubbed at their investiture, and the word *messiah* does not mean *the lathered-up one.* Thus, the proposed contemporizing of an ancient practice does not connect us with the biblical faith, and would have to be justified on the basis of change for the sake of novelty alone. Because the introduction of any change may arouse discomfort or displeasure, it is pointless to make changes that detract from baptism, rather than illuminate its biblical meaning.

How members of a particular congregation are best put in touch with the biblical heritage is a pastoral decision. What one congregation will embrace with enthusiasm may be rejected with hostility by another. In a Protestant parish that harbors no anti-ceremonial sentiment, and particularly in one with a significant number of persons of Roman Catholic or Orthodox heritage, the use of oil, new clothes, and a baptismal candle may fill a deep need. But in a parish that has a heavily anti-Roman Catholic bias, even the use of a bit more water than usual may raise cries of, "Papist!" Not that the threat of this should necessarily stop us, especially in the instance of applying enough water to allow its significance to be perceived by the senses. But the congregational reaction will determine how much preparation and explanation are required.

The various practices discussed in this chapter will therefore have to be assessed in relation to particular parish situations. In very few congregations will it be advisable to introduce all of the suggested innovations at once, and in some settings it may be unwise to introduce certain of them at all. In each case, we must decide, as best we can, which practices will facilitate the work of the Holy Spirit in communicating the good news to God's people, and which practices will only be a hindrance to that communication of the gospel.

## OCCASIONS FOR THE SERVICE

We have repeatedly indicated that baptism is an act of corporate worship that occurs with the congregation present. In most cases, this will mean that the celebration takes place within one of the stated Sunday services of worship. Implied within this is the fact that in all except the smallest parishes, several unrelated persons (including, perhaps, both infants and adults) may be baptized on the same day. This is as it should be. Because baptism is Christ's act in the church, we should in no way encourage what may appear to be an individualized service for one person or family at a time. Thus, the call for public baptism does not mean that in a parish with two dozen baptisms a year the sacrament will need to be administered every two or three weeks.

While baptism is appropriate to any Lord's Day (for each Sunday is a festival of his death and resurrection), certain occasions within the Christian year particularly commend themselves because of their meaning. We have noted that the vigils of Easter Day and the Day of Pentecost have been deemed especially suitable since ancient times. Where vigils are not practical, baptism may be transferred to the service of morning worship on that day. If for local reasons baptism on Easter Day is out of the question, the Sunday following may well be used.

A third occasion that is particularly felicitous is the observance of the Baptism of the Lord. In several denominations this is a recent addition to the calendar, being observed on the Sunday which falls between January 7 and 13 inclusive; but its origins rest in the theological meaning of Epiphany, the manifestation of God in Christ. Lessons for the day in the ecumenical lectionary center each year upon the meaning of Jesus' baptism by John.

A fourth appropriate time for baptism is All Saints' Sunday—the Sunday on or following November 1. While at first this may seem to be an odd time for the sacrament (since the day commemorates the death of all Christians who have gone before us), further reflection reveals a deep meaning. Through baptism, we are initiated into the whole company of Christ's people, living and dead; thus we are incorporated into the communion of saints. And sanctity is not an act of human determination but a gift of the Spirit. All Saints' Day celebrates the gracious, transforming work of Christ in those who faithfully respond to the indelible identity he places upon them through baptism.

These four baptismal occasions are not spaced evenly across the calendar, and as many as twenty-five Sundays fall between the Day of Pentecost and the first Sunday in November. When an occasion approximately in the middle of this long span is needed, those churches using the ecumenical lectionary will find these Sundays particularly appropriate:

Year A. Sunday with these readings:[1]
   Jeremiah 15:15-21. God's covenant faithfulness to Jeremiah.
   Romans 12:1-8. Living sacrifices; one body, many members.
   Matthew 16:21-28. Discipleship as taking up the cross.

Year B. Sunday with these readings:
   Isaiah 35:4-7a. Water in the wilderness.

James 1:17-27. First fruits of creation; doers of the Word.
Mark 7:31-37. The deaf hear and the dumb speak.

Year C. Sunday with these readings:
Exodus 32:1, 7-14. The golden calf and God's steadfast promise.
I Timothy 1:12-17. Christ's mercy overflows to sinners.
Luke 15:1-32. The lost coin, the lost sheep, and the lost son.

For most congregations, five baptismal occasions spaced every two to three months will provide sufficient opportunity for the administration of the sacrament. Times other than those suggested here may be designated, of course. The use of stated days for baptism will facilitate the scheduling of pre-baptismal education opportunities and related activities.

## THE SERVICE

Provided here is a general outline for a service of baptism within a service of corporate worship. No particular occasion is specified, but specific suggestions are given at points for some of the occasions discussed above. It is not possible to supply here a definitive commentary on the service; the purpose is to suggest an order, and to provide materials which supplement the denominational baptismal rite. For those who seek a more detailed rite of baptism than their own denominations provide, several recent revisions may be consulted for suggestions.[2]

The service begins with a form of gathering known as the entrance rite. A service of baptism will best commence in a manner to which the congregation is accustomed for regular Sunday services. If the liturgy normally begins with a responsive greeting, the following adaptation of I Peter 1:2-4, 6, 8 may be used.

May grace and peace be multiplied to you.
*Blessed be God for ever and ever.*
By God's great mercy we have been born anew to a living hope through the resurrection of Jesus Christ from the dead,
*to an inheritance which is imperishable, undefiled, and unfading.*

In this rejoice!
*We do rejoice with unutterable and exalted joy.*

Unfortunately most denominational hymnals suffer from a paucity of good baptismal hymns.[3] Until more ample poetic resources are available, a baptismal service may begin with a general hymn, or with a hymn related to the nature of the church. In particular, "Glorious Things of Thee Are Spoken" commends itself because of its imagery. Allusions to the last two chapters of The Revelation are found in its mention of the city of God with its streams of living water, its river that assauges all thirst; mention of the cloud and pillar of fire call to mind God's leadership in the wilderness after the Exodus, and the assurance of the promise given us at baptism is highlighted by the hymn's affirmation that God's Word cannot be broken. Finally, it is through divine faithfulness that we become the sons and daughters of God who are kept from fear of want.

During the season of Easter a very appropriate opening hymn is "Come, Ye Faithful, Raise the Strain" with its rich exposition of Exodus imagery in the opening stanza. Suitable for the Day of Pentecost are Charles Wesley's "See How Great a Flame Aspires" and Scott Brenner's "Descend, O Spirit, Purging Flame." Luther's text "To Jordan Came the Christ, Our Lord" is excellent for the Sunday of the Baptism of the Lord. Because of its allusion to Ephesians 4:5 at the end of each stanza, Edward Plumptre's "Thy Hand, O God, Has Guided" is especially suitable for All Saints' Day.[4]

If the entrance rite of the congregation usually includes confession, pardon, and a response of praise, the following can be employed for a baptismal service.

PRAYER OF CONFESSION
O God, our Creator:
Through your gracious love proclaimed in baptism
you have made us your sons and daughters.
But we rebel against your authority,
and do not live as responsible members of your family.
We envy those whom we judge to be more fortunate than we are,
while ignoring those whom we consider less privileged.

We hold at a distance brothers and sisters in Christ
　　who are different from us,
　　　and avoid those who challenge our narrowness.
Your zeal for justice and righteousness
　　finds only faint expression in our lives.
Drive out from among us all unworthy motives and desires,
　　and place within us a love which reaches out
　　　to all that you have made;
through Jesus Christ our Lord. Amen.


DECLARATION OF PARDON AND RESPONSE
　Receive the assurance of the Gospel:
　Once you were no people,
　　but now you are God's people.
　Once you had not received mercy,
　　but now you have received mercy.
　In Christ you are forgiven,
　　and are empowered to declare the wonderful deeds
　　　of the One who has called you
　　　　out of darkness into marvelous light.

　*Thanks be to God!*　　　　　　　　　　　(Based on I Peter 2:9-10)

Then a doxology may be sung. Or, instead of the sentence
response by the congregation and the doxology, the following
antiphonal reading based on Isaiah 12 may be used.

　　We give thanks to you, O Lord, for your anger is put aside.
　　　*You have given us consolation.*
　　We have trust now, and not fear.
　　　*For you, O Lord, are our strength and our song.*
　　God is our health and our hope.
　　　*And we will draw joyfully from the springs of salvation.*
　　Give thanks to the Lord.
　　　*Shout God's name.*
　　Sing to the Lord who has done marvelous things.
　　　*Declare them to the whole world.*
　　Cry out for joy and gladness, you who dwell in Zion.
　　　*For great in the midst of you is the Holy One of Israel.*

After the entrance rite there follows the Service of the
Word. If the lessons and sermon are normally preceded by a
prayer for illumination, the following may be used.

O God, who at the formation of the universe
    called light out of darkness:
Send brightness upon our way
      by the power of your Holy Spirit
    through the reading and preaching of your Word,
that we who are Christ's new creation
    may be faithful ministers unto the world;
through Jesus Christ our Lord. *Amen.*

Particularly on those occasions previously suggested for baptism, the lections provided in the three-year lectionary are suited for public reading and as the basis of the sermon for the day. When baptism occurs at other times, the assigned lections may also relate quite naturally to the sacrament. When this is not the case, two possibilities exist. Either the pericopes for the day should be respected, and the sermon will not focus upon baptism; or alternative readings may be used that do relate to baptism; some lectionaries make provision for such substitution.[5] Certainly it is preferable to choose other lessons rather than to do exegetical violence to the prescribed readings for the day.

It is hoped that the first five chapters of this book will provide the preacher with a wealth of material as the basis for preaching on baptism. Where baptisms are frequent, it is by no means mandatory that baptism be the subject of the sermon on each occasion. Certainly there will be opportunities also to refer to baptism in sermons on nonsacramental occasions. While the sermon on the day of baptism should be directed toward the candidates and their sponsors, care should be taken not to reinforce the all too prevalent notion that the congregation consists of mere spectators and eavesdroppers. Since every baptismal service we attend is an implicit renewal of our own baptism, the sermon is to be instructive and edifying to the entire assembly of believers.

Regardless of the subject of the sermon, the rest of the liturgy should be carefully planned in order to allow the amount of time for preaching to which the congregation is accustomed. If sermons are systematically shortened, over a period of time we convey the impression that preaching and the sacrament are competing forces, rather than complementary manifestations of the Word of God. Under no circumstances should the sermon be omitted on the occasion of baptism.

The sermon logically leads into the baptismal rite in the order of service; for baptism is both the continuation of the proclamation of grace and a form of response to that proclamation. Often the baptism of infants is placed as early in the order as possible, so that babies may then be taken from the congregation to the church nursery before the sermon. But the theological integrity of worship should not be compromised for the sake of peace and quiet in the assembly. Congregations need encouragement in accepting the presence of infants and children throughout worship. Where this is not readily achieved an alternative approach can be effective. Before the service begins, the infants can be taken to the nursery, and brought into the congregation after the sermon. A suitable hymn between the sermon and the baptismal rite can provide time for this to occur without undue distraction. Given suitable architectural arrangements, this could lead effectively into the traditional form of admission of candidates mentioned in chapter 2. Those coming for baptism knock at the door of worship area and are asked, "What do you ask of God's Church?" They respond, "Faith," and are admitted into the worshiping assembly. Then they may be introduced or presented to the congregation.

We come now to the rite of baptism proper. At a minimum this rite should include an act of renunciation of sin and of adherence to Christ; the use of the Apostles' Creed, preferably in its ancient interrogative form; a prayer of thanksgiving over the water; and the administration of the water. Denominational formularies that are defective in one or more of these elements may be supplemented by borrowing from contemporary liturgies that have these essential components.

In all cases, emphasis should be placed upon the water as being God's sign to us. In churches that do not have pools or flowing fountains, it is appropriate that the water be presented and poured into the font immediately before the prayer of thanksgiving over the water. The water may be brought from the midst of the congregation by a friend or relative of the candidates; or, if several unrelated persons are being baptized and implied favoritism presents difficulties, a designated official of the congregation may assume this responsibility. The water should be carried in a dignified container, and poured from a height sufficient to allow it to be seen and heard. That some people may be troubled if the water splashes onto the surrounding area may be a pastoral concern. There is, however, a theological concern in the other direction. It is in the very nature of water to splash and gurgle. That we should expect it to act in a more subdued manner in church is but another evidence of our failure to come to terms with creation as God's good work.

A prayer of thanksgiving over the water is traditional. This prayer highlights God's redemptive use of water in sacred history, and through its invocation of the Holy Spirit, indicates that water can be a means of grace through the contemporary action of God, yet is not a magical substance with independent powers. In those denominations where this prayer has dropped out of the liturgy, it should be restored. When a concise prayer is desired, those in recent Episcopal, Lutheran, and United Methodist rites may be used. When time permits, however, a more ample thanksgiving may be helpful. The following suggested prayer is punctuated by a congregational response (Ps. 8:1) which may be spoken in unison or set to music for singing. Where it is not practical to provide the congregation with the entire text of this prayer, the leader may say, "O Lord our God" in each instance, with the congregation instructed as to their part which follows.

> The Lord be with you.
> *And also with you.*
> Let us pray.
> *O Lord our God,*
> *how glorious is your name throughout the earth.*
> In the beginning your Spirit
>   swept across the waters,
>   bringing forth light and life
>     where chaos and death had reigned.
> When your people fell into sin,

you sent a flood upon earth,
but sheltered in the ark
  faithful Noah's family
  with the animals you had made,
that creation might be renewed.
After the deluge abated,
  you put in the heavens your rainbow,
    a sign of your covenant love.

*O Lord our God,*
*how glorious is your name throughout the earth.*

You gave your steadfast promise
  to Abraham and Sarah,
  and to their children for ever.
When their descendants were enslaved under Pharaoh,
  you brought them forth through the sea.
You led them by cloud and by fire,
  and gave them water in the wilderness.
You carried them over the Jordan
    into the land of Canaan,
  and made them a mighty nation.

*O Lord our God,*
*how glorious is your name throughout the earth.*

But again we fell into sin,
  though your prophets arose to warn us,
  and to dream of a new creation,
    a covenant written within.
And when all things were ready,
  you sent us your Anointed:
    Jesus, born of Mary,
    baptized for us in the Jordan.
You gave him the gift of your Spirit,
  that he might preach Good News to the poor.
He died at our hands,
  for our sin,
  and went to the place of the dead,
    to set the captives free
    by the power of his own resurrection.
He reigns with you in heaven
  as Lord over sin and death,

and sends us to baptize all nations,
    to make disciples of all.

*O Lord our God,*
*how glorious is your name throughout the earth.*

Pour out your Holy Spirit
    upon this, your gift of water,
    and upon those who in their baptism
        are buried and raised with Christ.
Anoint them as priests to the world;
make them your faithful people,
    who await your coming kingdom,
    yet already drink by grace
        the water of the river of life.
Create for yourself one family,
    sons and daughters born from above,
        united with saints of the ages:
    one Church on earth and in heaven.

*O Lord our God,*
*how glorious is your name throughout the earth.*

To you, O God most holy,
    be all glory for ever and ever.

*Amen.*

Baptism should be administered with clean, fresh water. Usually the water is administered three times, once as each Person of the Trinity is named. Where there is no compelling reason to use the Western formula, the work of Christ in the sacrament may be emphasized by employing the passive voice of the Eastern rites:

*Name,* you are baptized in the Name of the Father and of the Son and of the Holy Spirit. *Amen.*

## OR,

*Name* is baptized in the Name of the Father and of the Son and of the Holy Spirit. *Amen.*

The surname of the candidate is not used at the beginning of the formula, for it is an inherited family name, as distinct from the "given" (or "Christian") names. The Trinitarian language of the formula is to be used without alteration. Those who question this judgment should consider carefully what is at stake, and are referred to the appendix of this volume.

While we have insisted that God's action in baptism is not dependent upon the mode employed in administering the water, the modes do serve to highlight various meanings of the sacrament. Of the three modes commonly used, immersion and pouring have stronger biblical associations than does sprinkling. Immersion has christological significance. Whether or not the author had in mind a specific mode of baptism when writing Romans 6:3-4 and Colossians 2:12, certainly immersion is highly regarded today due to its similarity to the way corpses are buried in our culture. Pouring has a pneumatological (and therefore an ecclesiological) significance, for it reminds us of the pouring out of the Holy Spirit upon the church.

Sprinkling has less obvious biblical reference. Sometimes an appeal is made to Ezekiel 36:25, "I will sprinkle clean water upon you, and you shall be clean from all your uncleanness." Use of this text is indefensible exegetically, however. The prophet was talking about God's covenant relationship to Israel following the infidelity of the people to their covenant obligation. Ezekiel envisioned God cleansing the people who had been called to faithfulness generations ago. Thus, in this passage, sprinkling is connected with God's constant love in maintaining the covenant, not in initiating it. Nor, of course, did Ezekiel have baptism in mind, for this ritual cleansing rite came into Judaism during the intertestamental period. Finally, the verse from Ezekiel places such stress upon cleansing that it blinds us to other meanings of water in relation to baptism. If the passage can be used at all in connection with the baptismal covenant, it would be as a rationale for sprinkling persons during the rite of covenant renewal, not during baptism. Another possibility is to connect sprinkling with biblical references to the sprinkling of sacrificial blood, which thus relates this mode to the atoning work of Christ. But this significance is not readily apparent to most people.

Particularly in denominations that provide for sprinkling

in the rite of the renewal of the baptismal covenant, sprinkling as a mode of baptism may well be suppressed in order to prevent confusion between the sacrament itself and its renewal. Where sprinkling is retained as a mode of baptism, considerably more water should be employed than is usually used.

When pouring (or affusion, as it is sometimes called) is the chosen mode, an ample quantity of water should be laved over the candidate. Infants may be held with their heads over the font in a reclining or semi-reclining position. (They need not be held by the officiating clergy, but can be held by a parent or sponsor.) Water is then poured over the crown of the head so that the residue falls back into the basin. Adults stand or kneel before the font, face downward, so that water can be similarly poured over them. In some traditions a very large quantity of water is poured over the candidate, who stands upright. The rite is administered in this manner either out-of-doors, or with the candidate standing in a large basin, or on a surface impervious to water. After the baptism, the candidate must retire to a changing room, as is the case after immersion.

There is evidence of some renewed interest in the recovery of the traditional method of baptizing infants by dipping. In the Eastern Church the child is supported under the arms and lowered to the level of the chin into a deep container of water. In the West the practice evolved of holding the infant in a reclining position and dipping into a shallower basin, first the right side, then the left side, and finally face downward. Baptism by either method requires a large font; provision must be made for undressing the infants, drying them after baptism, and clothing them once again.

The anointing that may accompany baptism is done with olive oil. For the act of chrismation, the minister dips the right thumb into the oil and traces the sign of the cross upon the forehead of the baptized person with words such as, "You are sealed by the Holy Spirit in baptism and are marked as Christ's own for ever." Those present reply Amen. Where there is objection to the use of chrism but not to signation as such, the sign of the cross may be given without oil being used. Where resistance is to the sign of the cross rather than to the oil, the even more ancient sign of the fish may be traced with oil on the forehead; this is not the traditional practice, but may serve as an interim act until squeamishness about the sign of the cross can be overcome.

When a new garment is given, it can be a simple piece of clothing made by members of the congregation. For an infant, it may be a white tunic, and for an adult, either a tunic or a poncho-type garment. A cross, or fish, or other Christian symbol may adorn the clothing in a dignified manner. The garment may reflect the design of the church's funeral pall, where this is used, thereby linking Christ's grace at death and beyond to his action in baptism, and indicating that in baptism we experience the only death that really counts—death to sin. At the time of the vesting, those conferring the new garment may say, "Receive this new garment in token of the new life you have put on through your baptism."

A lighted candle, when given, should be a simple white candle, either unadorned or bearing a Christian symbol. The baptismal candle should not be confused with pink or blue decorated candles sold commercially for use on each birthday. When the candle is given, words derived from Matthew 5:16 may be spoken: "Let your light so shine before others [or, "before these children," when given to those presenting infants] that they may see your good works and give glory to God." Or the eschatological emphasis of baptism can be stressed by using the words of Matthew 25:13, "Watch [for the coming of the Lord], for you know neither the day nor the hour."

The baptismal candle is lighted from the paschal candle, where one is used. The paschal candle is a large candle lighted first at the Easter Vigil, and then at every service throughout the Great Fifty Days. It is a reminder of the pillar of fire that led the Hebrews in the wilderness. This Exodus light anticipates Christ, the light of the world, and the fire of the Holy Spirit who guides us. After the Day of Pentecost the paschal candle is placed at the font, and for the rest of the liturgical cycle is lighted only at baptisms and at funerals (when it is placed near the coffin as an assurance that Christ our light has preceded us in death, and through our baptism has brought us through death into his new life). Usually the paschal candle has a Greek cross inscribed on it; into the corners created by the intersection of the arms of the cross are inscribed the four numerals of the Year of our Lord (the calendar year) in which the candle is lighted. Above and below the cross (respectively) are an Alpha and an Omega. Thus, we are reminded that through baptism our fleeting lives are taken up and transformed by him who is the Lord of time, the beginning and the end of all things. All of this is brought home personally to the candidate when the baptismal candle is lighted from the paschal candle. The baptismal candle may be lighted in the home on each anniversary of baptism as a means of gratefully remembering baptism, and in the instance of those baptized at an early age, as a way of pointing forward toward a public affirmation of the baptismal covenant.

A difficulty with the recovery of practices such as the use of chrism, new clothes, and the baptismal candle is that a fascination with their novelty may obscure the centrality of water as God's sign. The purpose of the subsidiary rites is to explicate the sign, not to detract from it. Those who reform the baptismal service need to exercise judgment and restraint lest secondary things seem to be preeminent. On the other hand, the giving of the new clothes, or the candle, can be an effective way of driving out romantic practices, such as the custom of sprinkling a baby with a rosebud, and then giving the flower to the parents as a memento. A new pastor whose predecessor baptized with blossoms may wish to start the practice of giving instead the traditional tokens, pointing out the value of their symbolism in contrast with that of a cut flower that readly wilts, and therefore can hardly speak to us of the enduring new life in Christ.

Particularly when infants are baptized, opportunity should be given for other baptized children in the family to take part in the rite. Too often older children are left to sit alone in the pew as their parents and other adults go to the font: any resentment the older children already feel toward the newcomer in the family is thus increased. Baptized children of any age may join in the laying on of hands at baptism, where this practice is observed. An older child may be the water bearer; and younger children may bestow the new clothes or the candle (with some assistance from an adult).

For the most part, the entire service of baptism can be considerably declericalized. There is little in it that is strictly reserved to the clergy, even for the sake of decency and order. Members of the congregation of various ages should be given maximum opportunity to participate as evidence of the community baptism creates.

After the baptismal rite is concluded and the participants have returned to their places, intercessions may be offered, if these were not included within the denominational liturgy of baptism. Intercessions may be spontaneous, or may be prepared for each occasion. Or a litany such as this may be used:

Let us pray for the newly baptized.
Almighty God,
   you have engrafted your servants into Christ's church through
      baptism.
   Establish them that, being rooted and grounded in love,
      they may grow in grace
      and bring forth fruits of righteousness.
*Grant this gift of your Spirit.*

   Deliver from indifference and carelessness
      these new citizens of your kingdom.
   Deal patiently with them in times of disobedience and rebellion;
   and when they have fallen, restore them again by your great mercy.

*Grant this gift of your Spirit.*

   Cause your sign of water to be for these new Christians
      a perpetual testimony
      to your saving work and faithfulness.
   Spare them the anguish of deep doubt.
   Through the assurance of your eternal love,
      enable them to fulfill their ministry to others.

*Grant this gift of your Spirit.*

   We give thanks for these who have come
      to enlarge our company of believers.
   Help us, together with them, to serve you in trust and joy.
   Unite your whole  Church as one body,

that the world may come to acknowledge him
who is the  head of the church and the Lord of creation.

*Grant this gift of your Spirit through Jesus Christ our Lord. Amen.*

It is fitting for the intercessions to be led by a member of the congregation whenever possible.

Following the intercessions, the service proceeds with the exchange of peace, the offering of eucharistic gifts, and the eucharistic banquet, to which the newly baptized are admitted for the first time. As a mark of welcome, the new brothers and sisters in Christ should receive the bread and wine before others in the congregation. If a chalice of milk and honey is extended to the new Christians, they should drink it just before the communion elements are received.

After the Eucharist, the service properly concludes in a manner familiar to the congregation. An appropriate closing hymn is "Now Thank We All Our God." The dismissal with blessing may incorporate these words from the final portion of I Peter and apostolic blessing from the close of II Corinthians:

The God of all grace,
who has called you to eternal glory in Christ,
establish and strengthen you.

*To our God be dominion for ever and ever.*

The grace of the Lord Jesus Christ
and the love of God
and the communion of the Holy Spirit
be with you all. *Amen.*

While it is fitting for an informal reception (coffee hour, luncheon) to follow the service, it should be emphasized that the central corporate reception of the newly baptized occurs in their admission to the Lord's Table. Any further eating and drinking together derives its meaning from the eucharistic fellowship of the baptized.

The baptismal service as a whole requires careful planning. It is not unusual for rather complex situations to present themselves. Suppose, for example, that a new family in a community wishes to unite with the congregation. The woman is transferring membership from another parish. Her husband wishes to join on affirmation of faith, never having been baptized. A teen-age daughter has been baptized, and desires to make her first public renewal; and a young son is to be baptized. Thus in the same service there may be the baptism of an adult and of a child, the first public affirmation (confirmation) of a teen-ager, and reaffirmation of the baptismal covenant at the time of transfer. The service can be a marvelous testimony to the richness of baptism and the interrelation of its liturgical manifestations. Or the service can be an utter disaster—depending upon how much or how little planning is given to it, and how carefully the participants are instructed as to their roles. The attention given to the service will imply something about the way we regard the sacrament. Therefore, careful attention is needed in order that the congregation may perceive the importance of the rite, and be instructed in its meaning and edified by its celebration.

## THE ARCHITECTURAL SETTING OF BAPTISM

A foremost part of baptismal reform in many congregations will involve the size, design, and placement of the baptismal font or pool. A small furnishing of the same color wood as the chancel screen against which it snuggles (camouflaged even more by artificial palms, perhaps) reflects all too accurately our past indifference to the sacrament of initiation. Still less suitable is the small bowl that some congregations store in a cupboard, except on baptismal occasions. The font should be of ample size in order to demonstrate visually the importance of baptism, and to allow for the immersion of infants when that is desired. (See illustrations on pp. 175-76.)

The font should be located within the central liturgical space (as opposed to a side chapel or the narthex). There are two schools of thought about placement within the worship area, however. One suggests that the font be located near the central door as a reminder that we enter the church through baptism. The other says that the font should be located near the pulpit and the Lord's Table, as a visual expression of the unity of the Word preached and the Word proclaimed through the sacraments. Crucial to the decision about placement is the matter of visibility and accessibility. In buildings with fixed pews, locating the font behind the worshipers (at the main door) may preclude meaningful congregational participation in the baptismal liturgy. Few congregations will gladly stand for any period of time with their shins pressed against the seats of the pews in order that they may face the font. Even if they will, they may not be able to see much, unless the font is on a platform rather than at floor level. In a building with flexible seating, the matter is somewhat more easily resolved, though having to turn the chairs around to face the back for part of the liturgy can be annoying. Placement of the font at the door commends itself most readily in those situations where it is possible for the entire congregation to process from their seats to the baptistry for the rite.

If the font is in front of the worship area, its placement should visually indicate the importance of baptism. Those designing worship space may well consider having the Lord's Table in the center with the pulpit to one side; but instead of a lectern on the other side, a font of proportions sufficient to balance the pulpit may be used. (As fonts are generally too small to convey the importance of baptism, so pulpits frequenty are unduly large, and seem to suggest either that preaching is a superhuman feat, or that it is an exercise that calls for a fortress to hide behind.) The font should be surrounded by open space so that a number of people can conveniently gather round it during baptism. This openness will itself enhance the visibility and centrality of the font as one of the three foci within the liturgical space.

Where requests for the immersion of adults are likely to be frequent, building committees should give consideration to installing a baptismal pool, rather than having to borrow a facility or take chances with the weather. The pool, like the font, should be visually evident. There is something unsettling about a pool that cannot be seen except at baptism, because it is otherwise under a trap door, behind a drawn dossal curtain, or masquerades as a botanical garden. The site of baptism should be evident at every service of worship in order that those attending may gratefully remember their baptism whenever they assemble to praise God.

The importance of baptism may be conveyed visually through the use of stained glass, sculpture, tapestry, banners, and vestments, as well as by means of the sacramental furnishing themselves. Those who design and decorate worship space should give careful attention to the rich iconography of baptism. Images of creation, flood and rainbow, various waters related to the Exodus, the river Jordan, and the river of the heavenly Jerusalem lend themselves to incorporation in liturgical accoutrements, as do the more subtle symbols of the ichthus, the anchor, and the ship of the church.

What the eye sees is no less important in conveying theology and calling forth praise than what the ear hears. We face the challenge of facilitating experiences in sacramental worship that appeal to all the senses.

Worship is a means by which Christian faith is both formed and expressed. The liturgy shapes us even as we shape our forms of worship. The renewal of faith the church in our time yearns for, and the reform of worship substantive theology demands, are but one thing, inseparably bound. The reform of the liturgy is not a kind of tinkering with externals, while the weightier matters of the faith are ignored. Such reform has as its purpose the edification of the church in order that God's people may more effectively be witnesses in the world. Put another way: the reform of the liturgy of baptism grows out of a faithful response to God's grace proclaimed through baptism. Who will have one will have the other also.

This page and following page: Two views of a contemporary font of ample proportions. (Used by permission of Edward A. Sövik, of Sövik Mathre Sathrum Quanbeck Architects and Planners. Photos by Les Turnau.)

# EPILOGUE

By now it should be clear why Lucy was subjected to the confusion described in the prologue, and it should be equally clear why that confusion is so regrettable. I hope it is also evident that something can be done immediately and concretely to prevent such a travesty in the future.

For all of that, divine grace works in spite of our pitiable state of theological disarray. If Lucy had not been initiated into Christ's church five times, this book probably would not have been written—not by me, at least. For it was Lucy's telling of her story that sparked my interest in baptism nearly a decade and a half ago. Perhaps a brief account of my personal pilgrimage will encourage you to ask the kinds of questions I have had to raise, and will enable you to find new and delightfully unexpected meaning in your faith, as I have in mine.

I had served as a pastor for more than half a dozen years before hearing Lucy's story. I had regarded baptism as a tangential exercise—in the case of infants, a pious gesture on the part of devout parents; in the instance of adults, a public affirmation of faith by believers. As a pastor I had done almost all of the things I have condemned in this book. I had baptized babies with roses dipped into a bowl that was hidden in a cupboard most of the time. If I was not guilty of totally indiscriminate baptism, certainly I had come close to that. On one occasion I even rebaptized someone because she did not "feel" baptized. (To ease my conscience on that score, I did, at least, use the conditional formula.) I will not take on myself all of the blame for these errors. Sometimes I was simply following the bad advice or example of others; but the results were the same, and I had nowhere to go but up.

At about the same time that I heard Lucy's story, I listened to a pastor of my denomination expound on why he routinely rebaptized every youngster who completed confirmation class. That practice disturbed me, though I couldn't quite say why. I mentioned the matter to Professor Lowell B. Hazzard, who had been one of my mentors during seminary days; he recommended to me Donald Baillie's book, *A Theology of the Sacraments*. The reading of that work was the formal beginning of my adventure. A few years later another mentor, Professor Horton M. Davies, steered me toward F. D. Maurice's *The Kingdom of Christ*. Somewhere along the way I was introduced to P. T. Forsyth's *The Church and the Sacraments* by a good angel whose identity I have forgotten. (Fortunately, good angels are remarkably understanding and forgiving of feeble-minded professors.) In the course of other liturgical investigations, I happened upon Jean Daniélou's *The Bible and the Liturgy*. Many other books, articles, and discussions have helped to form the foundation of this volume; but the four works cited are the great cornerstones. The superstructure which I have built varies in detail and design from each book individually and all of them collectively. Yet without these four, nothing would have been built.

But enough of the masonic metaphor. Back to the pilgrimage motif. What I have learned about the meaning of baptism has radically altered my understanding of Christian faith and experience. I grew up in the Bible-belt of southern Illinois; there conversion, not baptism, was what really counted. I don't recall hearing anything at all about the meaning of baptism until I was an adult, except for superficial arguments about sprinkling infants versus immersing adults. As a teenager, I had a rather predictable religious experience, which for a number of years thereafter I regarded as the beginning of my Christian life. So far as I could tell then, my baptism in infancy had had nothing to do with that—or with anything else of spiritual importance. My baptism had been an empty form, I supposed; and my early years within the church were at best a prelude to what was to follow. I know first-hand what it is to boast about having been a church member for years before becoming a Christian.

My interpretation of things has been radically altered

because of what I have learned about baptism. I by no means despise the experience a week-long revival meeting produced in me during my junior year in high school. But I now believe that this experience was not the beginning of my life in Christ; nor was it of sturdy enough stuff to support a lifetime of faithfulness to God. That experience gave me a new sense of the reality of God's presence at a particular period in my life; but it was not the first time God had been present and active. And when I face difficulties and perplexity now, that subjective experience of late adolescence is far inferior to the assurance God gave me sixteen years earlier in the objectivity of the baptismal covenant. Increasingly I find that the sure promise of God extended to me, before I could begin to grasp its meaning even faintly, is far more helpful than any later emotional reaction on my part. When someone tells me how incomparable the experience of being baptized in adulthood was to them emotionally, I feel not the slightest sense of, "Gee, I wish that could have happened to me."

A few who read this may conclude that I have simply fallen from grace (though most who are of that persuasion probably closed the book long before now). I suggest instead that growth in grace is characterized precisely by the ability to reinterpret experience in the light of new spiritual insight. In this regard, I am a grateful heir of John Wesley. For on Sunday, January 29, 1738 (four months before his Aldersgate experience) Wesley wrote, "I, who went to America to convert others, was never converted to God." Years later he noted concerning that statement, "I am not sure of this." On the same date in 1738 he assessed himself to have been one alienated from God, a child of wrath, an heir of hell. But in 1774 he added to that assessment this notation, "I believe not"; and in his final edition of the *Journal* he deleted his 1738 self-evaluation entirely. As he matured in Christ, his earlier experience had to be reinterpreted.

For what is life if it is not a continual reappraisal of our past, in order that we may better understand the present, and have a secure hope for the future? And to their re-evaluation of their own history, Christians add God's history—what God has already done in Jesus Christ, and has promised through the gift of baptism. If we are not reinterpreting, then we are not growing; and when we do not grow, we frustrate the grace of God.

The meaning of my baptism has also brought me to a far deeper appreciation of the church than I had when I viewed it as a voluntary assemblage of the consciously converted (with some tares among the wheat, to be sure), or when somewhat later I viewed it primarily as the supply center for social activists. The theology of baptism has allowed me to hold in a creative tension the best of both of these views of the church; the church is a community of the committed who have a mission to the world. But baptism has also revealed the weaknesses in each of those positions and the necessary strengths which still other views of the church can contribute.

A new understanding of baptism has also brought me to a new evaluation of my call to the ministry. I can no longer view my vocational decision as a response to a unique and direct summons from God that conferred upon me a superior status within the church. The call of God, while to a very particular office in the church, was nevertheless related to the call that God gives to all of us through the sacrament of baptism; and it is precisely for this reason that ordination does not confer privilege upon a select group of Christians, but rather creates servants on behalf of the whole community of faith.

The theology of baptism has produced in me the conviction that neither my basic Christian faith nor my ministerial vocation can unrestrictedly be called a free choice. I am not a Christian, nor a member of the clergy, so much because I want to be, as because I am compelled to be. How much easier it would be to live the life of a hedonist, to be able to ignore the responsibility that the Christian faith puts upon each of us for the welfare of others! My baptism drives home to me the word of the Lord to his disciples, "You did not choose me, but I chose you and appointed you to go and bear fruit." Not that the Christian life is a dreary business with neither joy nor freedom in it. The paradox of the cross is this: that only in taking up what seems to be an intolerable burden laid upon us do we find true release. At the heart of that paradox is divine love, the love signified in the destructive-creative water through which we are buried, yet raised, with Christ, through which the gift of the Holy Spirit is made ours.

Finally, baptism has changed my perception of the future. The same God who claimed me before I could understand, through that very act gives me hope for a future that I cannot comprehend. At some point in the future death lurks. Its precise hiding place is as impossible to determine as its inevitability is impossible to deny. Will it come tomorrow in a bloody auto crash? Ten years hence, after some lingering malignancy? Fifteen or twenty years away in the terrifying cataclysm of a nuclear holocaust? There is no way of knowing. But ultimately it does not matter. For in baptism, I have died with Christ the only death that counts, and have already been raised to live in his new age.

That does not mean that I can speed down the highway with irresponsible abandon. Nor does it mean that a terminal illness would bring with it neither anxiety nor pain. Certainly it does not allow me to shrug off my responsibility to protest nuclear proliferation and international hostility. Yet, because God who gave me a promise in the past is faithful to the very end of the future and beyond, I can live today and tomorrow with confidence.

Luther was correct. When it is properly understood, there is no greater comfort on earth than this—that I am baptized. Because of this, I find an assurance even in ordinary water, and that sometimes under the most unlikely of circumstances—when I am bailing out my basement after a hurricane or howling because I have turned the wrong faucet in the shower stall. Even then, the water is a sign of the destructive-creative, saving power of God. Dashing across the quadrangle in the rain at the seminary where I teach, I sometimes shout to a drenched student, "Remember your baptism, and be thankful." Those who don't know me well take it as a bad joke. The rest know better.

If in this book I have not persuaded you to accept all of my opinions, that is a small concern to me, provided I have enabled you to start on a pilgrimage—on the kind of journey that will cause you to reexamine the good news, and to reassess your own experience of God's grace. It is a pilgrimage you need not fear. You walk in the land between the river of Eden and the river of the eternal City of God. Once you are headed in the right direction, there is no cause for ultimate anxiety. And if along the way you are caught without umbrella in a sudden shower, even then—particularly then—remember your baptism, and be thankful!

# NOTES

## PROLOGUE

1. I am grateful to Lucille Mangum of Wilmington, Delaware, for permission to use this true story, which she enjoys telling about herself.

## CHAPTER 1

1. People trained in contemporary methods of biblical study may have difficulty understanding the interpretation of the Old Testament found at points in the New Testament, particularly with uses of Old Testament passages in relation to baptism, a post-Old Testament practice. Therefore the following hermeneutical observations are provided.

(i) The early Christians had no Scripture except the Hebrew Bible, and even the exact content of that was not finally determined until the rabbinical council at Jamnia in A.D. 90. Since they were totally convinced that Jesus Christ fulfilled the Jewish hope, the first Christians readily found Christian meaning in the Old Testament.

(ii) This does not mean that they saw the incarnate Lord walking through the pages of the Old Testament. Paul's suggestion that the Hebrews were baptized and that the "rock was Christ" is not to be taken literally. The assumptions and meaning of I Corinthians 10:1-4 can be paraphrased in this way:

The love and faithfulness of God that we Christians have come to recognize most fully in Christ is not something novel. For God is the same, though revelations of God may assume new forms. What we have experienced in Christ, our forebears experienced (even if dimly) in the provision God made for them in the wilderness. We who do have the full revelation of God in the flesh find in the water of baptism a sign of God's power over sin and death and of God's guidance into freedom and life; our ancestors found the same power and goodness in the water of the sea and of the cloud. Thus in a certain sense, they were baptized, even as we are.

(iii) This way of looking at things gave rise to a hermeneutical method known as typology, in which parallels between the Hebrew

182

Scriptures and the Christian revelation are viewed, respectively, as anticipation and fulfillment (or, type and antitype). For example, I Peter 3:20-21 states that the water of baptism is the antitype (Gk. *antitypos*) of Noah's flood. The Jerusalem Bible catches the spirit, but expresses it by turning the Greek text on its head and saying that the water of the flood is a type of baptism. The RSV and many other versions do not even attempt to convey the technical type/antitype theology expressed in the Greek text.

The typological hermeneutic has value in maintaining the continuity of revelation, and makes it impossible to hold that the new covenant totally overthrows the Old Testament as Scripture for the church. While misuses of typology sometimes give the impression that there is nothing new in the New Testament, a sound typology makes this conclusion equally untenable. Inherent in this hermeneutical method is the principle that the new covenant fulfills the old, and does not simply duplicate it.

(iv) Typology is not to be confused with allegory. Allegory ignores the historical import of both Testaments by seeking a deeper "spiritual meaning" under the literal message of the text. Typology takes history seriously, for otherwise there is no possibility of anticipation and fulfillment.

Paul's reference to Hagar and Sarah in Galatians 4:24-25 is allegory, as he notes (and is one of the few instances of true allegory in the New Testament). The historical existence of the two women is irrelevant to Paul's point, which could have been made as readily by referring to two characters from mythology, or even to inanimate objects. But the Apostle's reference to the Exodus in I Corinthians 10:1-4 is not allegory; there historicity is assumed, and is required for the meaning (even if the historical accounts of the Exodus are not accurate to the degree Paul may have supposed).

Sound typology does not dismiss persons and events of the Old Testament as mere symbols or representations of something else, but sees God working through history toward an eschatological goal. As God's work advances, the divine purpose and victory become more apparent. What is seen dimly in Old Testament people and events can be seen more clearly in New Testament people and events, and will be revealed fully only at the end of time. One cannot set aside the historical persons and events by making them "mean" something symbolically.

(v) Within a typological hermeneutic, the Old Testament must be read at two levels: (a) what it meant originally, insofar as we can determine; (b) what it means for Christians who read it in the fuller light of the revelation of Jesus Christ. The slighting of either level destroys solid exegesis. To come to the Old Testament with too strong a historical-critical view is to find no Christian import in it; and to reject the historical-critical method is to fall into a mechanical view of inspiration that turns the Old Testament into a subtle form of allegory.

The two-level principle may be illustrated with reference to Psalm 23. The author said, and meant, "Yahweh is my shepherd." The Hebrew poet was not a crystal-ball gazer, and had no inkling there would ever be one referred to as "our Lord Jesus Christ." We must acknowledge this, and let the text exist on its own at one level. But in John's Gospel, Jesus is called the Good Shepherd; as Christians, we cannot read Psalm 23 as if John 10 did not exist. It is not only possible, but necessary, for us to see in Psalm 23 more than the author intended. The reason we lack nothing is that Christ is our shepherd. He prepares for us a eucharistic table; it is he who has preceded us through the valley of the shadow of death so that we need not fear evil. That is a typological reading of Psalm 23.

Only by keeping one foot firmly on the first level can we be sure we don't go off into irresponsible flights of exegetical fancy; but until we can be comfortable with the other foot on the second level, much of the richness of Scripture will be lost to us, as will be the church's appropriation of typology in hymns, prayers, and sermons. An understanding of typology is necessary for an appreciation of the ancient baptismal liturgy discussed in chapter 5.

A helpful analysis of typology is found in *Essays on Old Testament Hermeneutic,* edited by Claus Westermann, translated by James L. Mays (Richmond: John Knox Press, 1963). This work includes an essay by Bultmann rejecting typological interpretation; he is forcefully answered in essays by others, including Eichrodt, Goppelt, Lampe, and von Rad. In Roman Catholic circles, what I have here called the fuller sense of the Old Testament is identified by the Latin phrase *sensus plenior.*

Those who are troubled by what may seem to be a diminution of the historical-critical approach may find help in the reply Robert Frost is said to have made when someone asked him whether he objected when literary critics found more in his poetry than he intended. "No," he answered, "so long as they don't find less there than I intended." That is a good guide for exegetes.

2. Revelation 22:2 speaks of the healing of *ta ethnē,* usually translated as "the nations," which we tend to understand in geopolitical terms. But in Scripture, *ta ethnē* is an idiom meaning "the Gentiles"—those outside of God's covenant with Israel. Thus, the city of God is seen to be open to all who have been despised and regarded as outcasts.

3. Paul's term in I Corinthians 15:45 are usually translated as "the first Adam" and "the last Adam." Thus, Christ is seen as the final member of Adam's race; for being without sin, Christ cancels the penalty of sin by assuming it willingly. But Paul's title *eschatos Adam* is fuller than that, and could be translated as "the eschatological Adam," were that not so clumsy an expression. The title carries the connotation of one who begins a new order of things, the order of redemption. Thus, Christ is the pivot point: he is the last Adam who terminates the disaster of rebellion in the first creation, but he is also

the new Adam who begins the new creation through utter obedience to the will of God.

## CHAPTER 2

1. United Methodist readers will recognize that in addition to Scripture and tradition, the Wesleyan tradition considers experience and reason to be bases for faith. I have stressed the first pair because they are inherently more corporate, and because the other two rest upon them. Any individual may have a religious experience; but its Christian meaning can be determined only in the light of Scripture and tradition. Similarly, reason is an individual gift (though how reasonable a human being raised in total isolation would be, we can only guess); the Christian faith can be tested by reason but not invented by it. Theologians traditionally have distinguished between philosophy, which can be discovered by reason, and theology, which is dependent upon revelation. Through philosophy we may devise arguments for the existence, and even the benevolence, of God; but reason does not posit an incarnate God who dies an ignominious death in order that victory may appear in apparent defeat.

2. A possible syntactic linkage of repentance and faith may occur in Acts 20:21, for example. There a single definite article serves for the entire process. Luke writes of *"the* turning to God and faith in our Lord Jesus Christ." This nuance is usually lost in English translations. While too strong a case cannot be built on an isolated grammatical construction, in this instance the Greek usage seems to reflect a more general New Testament understanding about the essential unity of repentance-faith.

3. After having used the statement of the epileptic's father ("I do believe; help the little faith I have") in connection with baptism for a number of years, I recently discovered the following comment in which Alan Richardson links the entire pericope (Mark 9:14-29) to sacramental practice:

St. Mark probably meant [this pericope] to be a story that could be used by his catechists in their instruction about baptism. An exorcism takes place, as we held to take place in every baptism. The faith of the sponsor was necessary before the saving action can begin. The disciples have no power of themselves to effect the work; Jesus alone is the true minister of baptism. And death and a rising take place: "The child became as one dead, insomuch that the more part said, He is dead. But Jesus took him and raised him up; and he arose *(anestē);* Jesus is the resurrection and the life. Finally the importance of prayer at baptism is stressed (and a later age adds fasting). [Alan Richardson, *An Introduction to the Theology of the New Testament* (New York: Harper & Brothers, 1958), p. 360.]

If Richardson is correct, one can hardly avoid speculating about the effect of this pericope upon the development of the question, "What do you ask of God's church?"—particularly since in the ancient church (as in recent Roman Catholic liturgical reform) the query appeared in the rite of admission to the catechumenate rather than in the baptismal rite proper.

4. For a helpful discussion of the meaning of the term *world* in Johannine literature, see *The Anchor Bible,* vol. 29, William Foxwell Albright and David Noel Freedman, gen. eds.; *The Gospel According to John (i-xii),* introduction, translation, and notes by Raymond E. Brown, S. S. (Garden City, N.Y.: Doubleday & Co. 1966), pp. 508-10.

## CHAPTER 3

1. A crucial point of difference between those who accept, and those who reject, sacraments is this: sacramentalists stress the activity of God from which human response springs. Those who reject sacraments stress human response as a testimony of faith. The former view corresponds roughly to the inclusive position and the latter to the exclusive position. Theoretically, at least, it is possible to maintain a sacramental view while insisting that baptism is only for committed adults. While to my knowledge no denomination espouses such a synthesis, some Baptists and members of the Christian Church [Disciples of Christ] seem to be moving in the direction of regarding baptism as a sacrament while retaining their historic restrictions concerning who may be proper candidates.

2. The inclination of some believers' baptist groups to baptize those who can hardly be considered mature is justifiably criticized from within those groups, as is clear in this statement by a European Baptist: "It is generally known that a number of Baptist congregations in the USA baptize children as 'believers' by immersion. In 1976 Southern Baptists baptized 35,562 children under eight years of age. This is 'frowned' upon by most non-American Baptists, but it is also criticized from within the Southern Baptist context." [Thornwald Lorenzen, "Baptists and Ecumenicity with Special Reference to Baptists," *Review and Expositor,* LXXVII, 1, p. 42, n. 1.]

3. The pertinent documents in this debate are:

Kurt Aland, *Did the Early Church Baptize Infants?* trans. G. K. Beasley-Murray (Philadelphia: Westminster Press, 1963).

Karl Barth, *The Teaching of the Church Regarding Baptism,* trans. Ernest A. Payne (London: SCM Press, 1954).

Oscar Cullman, *Baptism in the New Testament,* trans. J. K. S. Reid (Chicago: Henry Regnery Co., 1950).

Joachim Jeremias, *Infant Baptism in the First Four Centuries,* trans. David Cairns (Philadelphia: Westminster Press, 1960).

4. Parental anxiety about the status of children in those churches that do not baptize infants expresses itself liturgically in two forms: (1) the use of a liturgy, popularly known as the dedication of infants, which often has an undeniably sacramental flavor; (2) the progressive

lowering of the age at which people are baptized to the point that it is not uncommon for three- and four-year-olds to be regarded as believers for this purpose. Some observers attribute the second development to a need to show statistical church growth, but that alone likely does not account for the phenomenon.

5. For a recent defense of rebaptism, see Earl L. Langguth, "Why I Rebaptize," The *Circuit Rider*, 3 (June 1979): 11. Letters to the editor in a subsequent issue of this United Methodist clergy journal revealed that, while the author had some perceptive critics, he is by no means alone in his views and practices; *ibid.* (September 1979): 17-19.

6. The realization that, by definition, one can be initiated only once lies behind the little understood word-play in the dialogue of Jesus and Nicodemus in John 3:1-15. The pericope, which many scholars regard as being clearly baptismal on the basis of 3:5, centers on the Greek term *anōthen,* a word that means both *from above* and *again.* Jesus says, "You must be born *anōthen.*" Likely the writer intends the meaning here to be *from above.* But Nicodemus is depicted as being somewhat obtuse; supposing that Jesus means rather *again,* this inquirer comments on the impossibility of entering the womb a second time. Thus Jesus instructs him on the nature of the heavenly kingdom. The only way to be born *again* is to be born *from above* by the water and the Spirit. The church came to understand that the birth given through baptism is as unrepeatable as physical birth. You can't be born *anōthen anōthen* (from above again).

7. The movement toward the recognition of the sacramental baptism of infants by those in churches that historically baptize only adults is seen in the "Report of the Consultation With Baptists" sent to the Faith and Order Commission of the World Council of Churches. The report of the consultation, which was held March 28–April 1, 1979, states:

> Although the divide between paedo-baptist churches and the Baptists evidently remains, there are signs of bridge-building from both sides. Conversations revealed that for some from both groups the bridge is sufficiently complete to allow mutual recognition of each other's practices. For others the gap remaining has narrowed sufficiently to permit mutual respect and growing understanding of the reasons for the different practices. . . .
>
> [One point] of agreement within the consultation [is]: The acceptance that believers' baptism is the most clearly attested practice of the New Testament, together with the recognition that infant baptism has developed within the Christian tradition and witnesses to valid Christian insights.
>
> *Review and Expositor,* LXXVII (Winter 1980): 101.

As a participant in the consultation, I can report that a number of Baptists (who represented different Baptist denominations from four continents) felt comfortable with the concept of baptism as an act of God, not merely as a testimony of human faith; and many of these persons were equally willing to use the term *sacrament* in connection with baptism.

8. See J. G. Davies, *The Architectural Setting of Baptism* (London: Barrie and Rockliff, 1963), chapter 1.

9. John Wesley, *The Journal of The Rev. John Wesley, A.M.*, ed. Nehemiah Curnock. 9 vols. (London: The Epworth Press, 1938) I:476 [entry of May 24, 1738]. On subsequent days Mr. Wesley recorded similar feelings of ambivalence; e.g., "I waked in peace, but not in joy," *ibid.*, I:479 [May 28, 1738].

10. Consultation on Church Union, *An Order of Thanksgiving for the Birth or Adoption of a Child* (n.p., 1980). The Episcopal Church, "A Thanksgiving for the Birth or Adoption of a Child," *The Book of Common Prayer* (New York: The Church Hymnal Corporation and The Seabury Press, 1979), pp. 439-445.

11. Tertullian, *Homily on Baptism [De Baptismo]*, trans. with intro., Ernest Evans (London: S.P.C.K., 1964). p. 35 [c. 17].

12. While baptism has been held to be necessary for salvation, the actual administration of the rite has not been an absolute requirement. Confronted with the extreme case of someone who is dying in isolation and can find no available minister, it is allowed that the person may receive baptism "by intention"; God recognizes that the desire cannot be fulfilled, therefore the desire itself suffices. In the early era of the church, catechumens who were martyred before the actual administration of the water were said to have been baptized in their own blood.

13. Peter Taylor Forsyth, *The Church and the Sacraments* (London: Longmans, Green, & Co., 1917), pp. 177-78, 205. Italics Forsyth's.

14. *Ibid.*, pp. 181-82.

## CHAPTER 4

1. The neglect of forms of renewal has not been absolute. In the Roman Catholic tradition, the sprinkling of water upon the congregation (the *asperges*) at the beginning of High Mass, and the sprinkling of the coffin at the Requiem Mass, were intended to be reminders of baptism and its perpetual significance: through baptism the Lord brings his people to the eucharistic feast, and leads them through the valley of the shadow of death to the table that he has prepared in the eternal home. The making of the sign of the cross after dipping the fingers into water at the entrance of the place of worship also served to remind the faithful that they enter the community of faith through baptism, and have a continuing covenant within that community.

On the Protestant side, John Wesley adapted for Methodists a covenant renewal service originated by the Puritan, Richard Alleine. The service sets forth the need for perpetual renewal in a forceful way. Unfortunately it does not explicitly relate that renewal to the baptismal covenant, though in practice an implicit relationship exists whenever the covenant rite leads into the celebration of the Eucharist.

Many Protestants have an all-too-unrecognized form of renewal in the use of Apostles' Creed at the Eucharist and other services. Since this statement of faith originated as a baptismal creed and has been so retained in most initiation rites, its use at other times constitutes a form of baptismal renewal.

2. Contemporary Methodists usually explain the welcome granted to children at the Eucharist by recalling Wesley's view that the Supper is a converting ordinance, not merely a confirming ordinance. In contrast to the high Calvinists of his day who restricted communion to those who had clear indication of their status as the elect of God, Wesley held that the Eucharist is a means of grace through which those unsure of their salvation may find assurance. In their zeal for open communion, Methodists have frequently outrun Mr. Wesley, however. All of the "seekers" in Wesley's day were baptized, since the administration of baptism to infants was general in the Church of England; Wesley further assured the seriousness of all who came to the Table by issuing communion tokens only to those adults who participated in prayer and study groups. The modern Methodist notion that the Eucharist is open to all persons, baptized or not, is un-Wesleyan, no matter how well-intentioned it may be; the reception of communion by baptized children, however, is more clearly in the Wesleyan spirit.

The practice of Orthodoxy and Methodism with respect to the communion of the young has renewed pertinence in answering certain kinds of arguments against the baptism of infants. For example, Paul K. Jewett contends that the refusal to admit baptized infants to communion demonstrates the insupportable nature of infant baptism from a covenant perspective [*Infant Baptism and the Covenant of Grace* (Grand Rapids: William B. Eerdmans, 1978)]. In implying an absolute inconsistency by churches which baptize infants, Jewett overlooks the practice both of Orthodoxy and of Wesleyans; these groups, taken together, constitute a quite significant proportion of paedo-baptist Christians. He also treats insufficiently the fact that communion of infants disappeared in the West before the Reformation for reasons not directly related to the theology of the Eucharist vis-à-vis baptism, and that the Reformers continued the late medieval innovation without clearly understanding its origin or purpose.

3. *New York Times*, April 9, 1972.

## CHAPTER 5

1. Water is not explicitly mentioned in Luke's sparse account of Jesus' baptism (3:21-22); but clearly the reader is to make the association between "had been baptized" and the earlier statement of John the Baptizer in verse 16, "I baptize you with water."

2. Further evidence that the Gospel writers saw Jesus as the new Moses is found, for example, in Luke's account of the Transfigura-

tion. As in the other Synoptics (Matt. 17:3; Mark 9:4), Jesus converses with Moses and Elijah (Luke 9:30). That is, he fulfills the Law and the Prophets—the two great bodies of Scripture accepted as canon by common consent prior to the final determination of the Hebrew canon at Jamnia in A.D. 90. But Luke makes an addition concerning that conversation: Jesus is discussing "his departure, which he was to accomplish at Jerusalem" (Luke 9:31). What the RSV translates somewhat insufficiently as "departure" is in the Greek *exodus*. Luke's choice of the term can hardly be accidental, particularly in light of the concurrence of the Feast of Passover and the sacrifice of the Lord as reported in the passion narratives, and in light of the effect this concurrence had upon early Christian thought and worship. The Lord's passage from death to life is the new exodus, by means of which the new Moses leads his people to freedom.

3. *The Anchor Bible*, vol. 37, William Foxwell Albright and David Noel Freedman, gen. eds.; *The Epistles of James, Peter, and Jude*, introduction, translation, and notes by Bo Reicke (Garden City, N.Y.: Doubleday & Co., 1964), pp. 106-7, 139.

4. Readily available collections of the ancient documents (including pertinent sections of Justin's *Apology* and *The Apostolic Tradition*) are: *Baptism: Ancient Liturgies and Patristic Texts*, Andre Hamman, O.F.M., ed. (Alba Patristic Library, 2), trans. Thomas Halton (Staten Island, N.Y.: Alba House, 1967).

E. C. Whitaker, ed., *Documents of the Baptismal Liturgy*, 2nd ed. (London: S.P.C.K., 1970).

5. We have many examples of such mystagogy, as the post-baptismal instruction is called, from the writers of the early period of the church. See, for example, Philip T. Weller, ed., *Selected Easter Sermons of Saint Augustine* (St. Louis and London: B. Herder Book Co., 1959).

6. On this point see *Theological Dictionary of the New Testament*, vol. IV, Gerhard Kittel, ed. (Grand Rapids: William B. Eerdmans Publishing Co., 1967), 241-50.


## CHAPTER 6

1. Augustine's regard for the sacraments apart from the moral character of the minister led to the principle of *ex opere operato*, a phrase which has been more caricatured by Protestants than understood. The intention behind the concept was to stress the objective character of God's work in the sacrament, so that the rite is not seen simply as a subjective or psychologically determined event. The formula does not mean, however, that God's work is automatic and irresistible; it is understood that sacraments are effective only to those who desire their effects and put no barrier in the way. This is consistent with the biblical understanding of the term *sign:* A

sacrament is not a miracle which will persuade or impose itself upon the skeptic, but neither is it simply an affirmation of faith on the part of the believer. It is God's gift to those who will receive it, and its efficacy rests upon divine faithfulness.

2. Over a period of centuries after Augustine, problems related to the removal of original guilt at baptism, and to the existence of actual sin following baptism, gave rise to the notion that there are two levels between heaven and hell. Hell was for the unbaptized; but there was reluctance to consign to hell unbaptized infants who had not yet committed actual sin. It was said that for their sake a state of limbo exists—nothingness, as distinct from active punishment. Further, since most adults during their lives would not do enough acts of penance to cover their actual sins, at death they could not go directly to heaven, even though baptized. For them was provided purgatory, where through limited suffering they could be purged of their remaining actual guilt. This system produced a legalistic attitude toward baptism that diminished the richness characteristic of the sacrament in the early centuries.

3. Immersion certainly was not unknown among early Anabaptists, but insistence upon this mode came slowly, and worked its way back to the older Anabaptist groups on the continent after British Baptists began to require it. There are interesting evidences of the lack of rigidity among the early Anabaptists and British Baptists. To this day Mennonites in the United States employ pouring as a mode; being a conservative group, they have retained the early attitude of continental Anabaptists. In 1673, the noted leader of the British Baptists, John Bunyan, published *Differences in Judgment about Water Baptism no Bar to Communion;* he held that neither the mode of baptism nor even opinions about the necessity of it should hinder sincere Christians from joining in fellowship together around the Lord's Table.

4. In Anglicanism, the controversy over whether baptism or confirmation confers the seal of the Spirit erupted in the late nineteenth century, when F. W. Puller and A. J. Mason argued that confirmation is the necessary seal that completes Christian initiation. The debate was resumed in our century with Gregory Dix and L. S. Thornton taking up the view of Puller and Mason; their chief critic was G. W. H. Lampe.

Because the separation of confirmation into a later sacrament has sometimes been justified on the basis of Acts 8:14-17, it is helpful here to look at that passage itself and in the context of other references in Acts to water, the laying on of hands, and the gift of the Spirit.

To the point at which the account in question begins (Acts 8:4), the mission of the church has been only to Jews. Now Phillip (not the apostle, but the deacon mentioned in 6:5) has preached among the Samaritans, who were regarded by Jews as heretics. Yet Samaritans believed, and Philip baptized them. When the apostles heard this, they sent John and Peter to pray with the Samaritans that they might receive the Holy Spirit, which they did at the laying on of hands. If this is to be regarded as confirmation, it is that only in a very restricted sense. The apostles confirmed an irregular action performed by a deacon outside the community of faith in Jerusalem. Heretofore in Acts, baptism had been administered only by the apostles and only to Jews. On these grounds alone, the passage seems to provide little precedent for the life and order of the church centuries later.

But the account also needs to be examined in relation to its context. Luke describes various relationships between the administration of water, the laying on of hands, and the reception of the Spirit in terms of the sequence in which these occur. Therefore it is sometimes suggested that Luke had no clear theology about the relationship of these events, or that he was expressing in another way the insight of John 3:8 that the wind [spirit] blows where it wills, and is not subject to precise formulations. Other commentators suggest that Luke somewhat ineptly combined two traditions—an early, charismatic one in which the Spirit is given before the water, and a later, more ecclesial one in which the Spirit is given with or after the water. If any of these suggestions is true, then the account concerning the Samaritans can be read in relative isolation. I want to suggest, however, another possibility which, as far as I know, is my own interpretation.

In light of Luke's interest in the growth of the church's self-understanding of God's mission for it, it is possible that there is a deliberate pattern to the various relationships Luke records between water, hands, and Spirit. To understand this possibility, we need to rid ourselves of mechanical ideas about the imparting of the Spirit which read medieval theology back into Scripture. Let us think, instead, of the church as the Spirit-filled community that welcomes new members into its company through the laying on of hands as a sign of corporate sharing in the work of the Spirit. That is, when the apostles lay hands on others, they do this as representatives of the community, not as individuals who somehow mechanically transmit divine power to new members. Thus the laying on of hands focuses, not upon apostolic authority as such (a concern that arose only later), but upon the community of faith as the sphere within which the Spirit works, and is made known through the interaction of the whole people of God. If this interpretation can be allowed, the sequence of events in Acts takes on new meaning.

The account of the conversion of the Samaritans is the first explicit mention in Acts of water, hands, and Spirit together. Here the church is uncertain about its relationship to its ancient opponents, the Samaritans. Philip, somewhat brashly perhaps, has baptized Samaritans. Now the apostles must determine whether these converts can legitimately be welcomed into the community of the Spirit. Hence, the laying on of hands follows the administration of water by a significant interval.

The next mention of water-hands-Spirit is in Acts 9:17-19. Saul of Tarsus, a devout Jew, does not present the same kind of problem the Samaritans did. But there is another difficulty; although a devout Jew, Saul has been a notorious enemy of the church. Ananias, representing the Christian community in Damascus, lay hands on Saul to restore his sight. But verse 12 must be read in a double sense in light of the words of Ananias in verse 17; both verses refer to the restoration of sight, but the latter adds being "filled with the Holy Spirit." The New Testament refers to baptism as enlightenment, and Paul's physical blindness is but an indication of spiritual depravity. The return of Paul's sight is evidence of enlightenment in Christ. Ananias, willing to extend to another member of the House of Abraham the traditional laying on of hands (v. 12), is nevertheless hesitant to administer baptism until the physical evidence of spiritual change has been given by God. That is, the community of the Spirit approaches a fellow Jew more readily than it approaches a Samaritan; it is not necessary for the apostles to send a delegation from Jerusalem, for a local disciple will serve in this case. Yet what the community does, it does in hope, awaiting the evidence of the work of the Spirit before administering the rite that most clearly distinguishes the church from the House of Abraham.

Having worked through its mission to heretical Samaritans and to a recalcitrant Jew, the church next must work through its calling to the Gentiles. Thus when Peter is sent to the house of Cornelius, we encounter mention of the Spirit and of water but, significantly, not of the laying on of hands. For here the church is exceedingly timid. So hardened are the apostles in their view of the Gentiles that nothing short of direct divine action will accomplish the reception of these outsiders into the community of the Spirit. Thus the Spirit is given directly in order to persuade Peter (and, subsequently, the church in Jerusalem) that Gentiles may indeed enter the community through baptism (Acts 10:1–11:18). In effect, a reluctant church is forced to share the Spirit-in-community.

There is only one other mention of water-hands-Spirit in Acts. In 19:1-7 Paul encounters in Ephesus some twelve disciples who had been baptized with John's baptism, but knew nothing of the Holy Spirit. Paul baptizes them in the name of Jesus, places hands upon them, and they receive the Spirit. Probably, like Apollos, they were Jews; for they were disciples of John, and attended synagogue with Paul. But even if they were not Jews, by now the church had come to realize the full extent of its mission, and the order of water-hands-Spirit in a single initiatory rite was established.

If I am correct in analyzing Luke's purpose and method, only this latter sequence stands as a possible norm for the church; Acts 8:14-17 is totally irrelevant as support for a separate episcopal sacrament added to baptism. Indeed, Luke seems to suggest that the church is to approach all who desire to enter it with a spirit of openness, not with suspicion (as it did the Samaritans), hesitation (as it did Saul of Tarsus), or a recalcitrant refusal to share the blessings of the Spirit-given-through-community (as in the case of Cornelius). If anything, then, Acts sets a precedent for a unified act of initiation, not for a separated sacramental act of confirmation administered by bishops only.

5. The fact that the revivalists frequently exalted personal experience over education does not mean that they opposed all education or social progress. Quite the contrary. The revival spawned hundreds of church colleges and academies. Charles G. Finney, the noted evangelist and chief apologist of the movement, was lukewarm toward classical theology; yet he founded, and became the first president of, Oberlin College, an institution that was anti-slavery and pro-feminist in philosophy. Nevertheless, revivalists often distinguished between the benefits of general education and the perils of theological education. To this day some students come to seminary having been warned to be on guard, lest they lose their faith there!

## CHAPTER 7

1. Howard Hageman attributes this metaphorical axiom to G. Van der Leeuw, but does not give a precise citation for it. *Pulpit and Table.* (Richmond: John Knox Press, 1962), p. 15.

2. For a recent example of the kind of misunderstanding that can arise from the statement that sacraments convey grace, see Vernard Eller's *In Place of Sacraments: A Study of Baptism and the Lord's Supper* (Grand Rapids: William B. Eerdmans, 1972). Eller's misunderstanding of sacramental theology results in a caricature, rather than an explication, of that theology. It is not difficult, however, to see how Eller and others could be misled by the way sacramental theology has frequently been stated.

3. Lutheran and United Methodist congregations wishing to pursue joint study of baptism will find a helpful resource in the pamphlet, "A Lutheran-United Methodist Statement on Baptism," which may be ordered free, except for postage, from the Service Center, 7820 Reading Road, Cincinnati, Ohio 45234. This document is a report of an ecumenical dialogue team, and is designed for use in local churches. It is to be hoped that similar interdenominational materials will be developed in the future by other groups to facilitiate ecumenical study experiences.

## CHAPTER 8

1. The lections given are from the United Methodist Lectionary, 1979 revision. Corresponding pericopes are found in the recent

lectionaries of a number of denominations, but with some slight variation as to assigned dates. In the United Methodist and Episcopal calendars, the days suggested fall as follows:

Year A—Sunday between August 28 and September 3, inclusive.
Year B—Sunday between September 4 and September 10, inclusive.
Year C—Sunday between September 11 and September 17, inclusive.

In the Lutheran, Presbyterian, and United Church of Christ systems, these days are the fifteenth, sixteenth, and seventeenth Sundays after Pentecost, respectively, and fall within a wider range of time due to the movable character of the Day of Pentecost. While it may seem desirable to use the same liturgical day for baptism each year, the content of these sets of lections casts significant weight in the direction of a system less neat than that.

2. Recent service books that are helpful resources include:

EPISCOPAL
*The Book of Common Prayer* (New York: The Church Hymnal Corporation and The Seabury Press, 1979)
Holy Baptism, pp. 298-314.
Confirmation, pp. 412-19.
The Great Vigil of Easter, pp. 284-9.

LUTHERAN (joint)
*Lutheran Book of Worship* [Ministers Desk Edition] (Minneapolis and Philadelphia: Augsburg and LCA Board of Education, 1978)
Holy Baptism, pp. 308-12; notes, pp. 30-31.
Affirmation of Baptism, pp. 324-27; notes, pp. 35-36.
Service for Vigil of Easter, pp. 143-53; notes, pp. 24-25.

PRESBYTERIAN (joint)
*The Worshipbook* (Philadelphia: Westminster Press, 1972)
The Sacrament of Baptism, pp. 43-47.
The Commissioning of Baptized Members, pp. 48-52.

ROMAN CATHOLIC
*The Rites* (New York: Pueblo Publishing Co., 1976)
Christian Initiation, pp. 3-334.

UNITED CHURCH OF CHRIST
*The Hymnal* (Philadelphia: United Church Press, 1974)
The Sacrament for the Baptism of Infants, pp. 29-31.
The Order of Confirmation, pp. 31-34.

UNITED METHODIST CHURCH
*A Service of Baptism, Confirmation, and Renewal* [Supplemental Worship Resources 2] (Nashville: United Methodist Publishing House, 1980]

*From Ashes to Fire: Services of Worship for the Season of Lent and Easter with Introduction and Commentary* [Supplemental Worship Resources 8] (Nashville: Abingdon, 1979)

   Easter Vigil or the First Service of Easter, pp. 165-201.

3. A commendable selection of baptismal hymns is, however, to be found in the *Lutheran Book of Worship* [Pew Edition] (Minneapolis and Philadelphia: Augsburg and LCA Board of Publication, 1978).

4. "Come, Ye Faithful" is available in a number of hymnals. Wesley's hymn is no. 464 in the United Methodist *Book of Hymns* (Nashville: The Methodist Publishing House, 1966) [early printings entitled *The Methodist Hymnal*]. Brenner's hymn is No. 353 in the Presbyterian *Worshipbook;* Luther's hymn is No. 79 in the *Lutheran Book of Worship* (Pew Edition). Plumptre's text, not readily available, is given here both in its original form and in my contemporary revision. The text is in 7.6.7.6. iambic, and may be sung to familiar tunes such as "Aurelia" and "Lancashire."

## ORIGINAL

Thy hand, O God, has guided
thy flock from age to age;
the wondrous tale is written
full clear on every page;
our fathers owned thy goodness,
and we their deeds record;
and both of this bear witness,
one church, one faith, one Lord.

Thy heralds brought glad tidings
to greatest and to least;
they bade men rise and hasten
to share the great King's feast;
and this was all their teaching,
in every deed and word,
to all alike proclaiming
one church, one faith, one Lord.

When shadows thick were falling
and all seemed sunk in night,
thou, Lord, didst send thy servants,
thy chosen sons of light.
On them and on thy people
thy plenteous grace was poured,
and this was still their message:
one church, one faith, one Lord.

And we, shall we be faithless?
Shall hearts fail, hands hang down?
Shall we evade the conflict,
and cast away the crown?
Not so; in God's deep counsels

## CONTEMPORARY REVISION

Your hand, O God, has guided
your flock from age to age;
the wondrous tale is written
full clear on every page;
our forebears owned your goodness
and we their deeds record;
and both of this bear witness,
one church, one faith, one Lord.

Your heralds brought glad tidings
to greatest and to least;
they bade each rise and hasten
to share Christ's holy feast;
and this was all their teaching,
in every deed and word,
to all alike proclaiming
one church, one faith, one Lord.

When shadows thick were falling
and all seemed sunk in night,
you, Lord, did send your servants,
the bearers of your light.
On them and on your people
your plenteous grace was poured,
and this was still their message:
one church, one faith, one Lord.

[no alteration needed]

some better thing is stored;
we will maintain unflinching
one church, one faith, one Lord.

Thy mercy will not fail us,
nor leave thy work undone;
with thy right hand to help us,
the victory shall be won;
and then by men and angels
thy name shall be adored,
and this shall be their anthem:
one church, one faith, one Lord.

Your mercy will not fail us,
nor leave your work undone;
with your right hand to help us,
the victory shall be won.
By those on earth and angels
your name shall be adored,
and this shall be their anthem;
one church, one faith, one Lord.

5. Lections for baptism are found in *The Book of Common Prayer* (1979), p. 928. The *Lutheran Book of Worship* [Ministers Desk Edition] contains an even fuller set of lections, together with prayers and other propers, pp. 188-89.

# APPENDIX

## CONCERNING THE USE OF THE
## TRINITARIAN FORMULA

The Trinitarian baptismal formula is in a certain amount of disfavor these days because of the sexist nature of its references to the Father and the Son. While the weight of tradition and the importance of the catholic formula to ecumenical relations are worthy considerations for retaining the Trinitarian formula, these are not the major concern for its continued use. The principal concern has to do with theological matters implied in this formula, and not implied (indeed, sometimes possibly excluded) in suggested substitutions such as "in the Name of the Creator, the Redeemer, and the Sustainer."

At the time of initiation into the Christian faith we need to say as much as we possibly can about God, in as concise and as memorable a way as is practical. Unfortunately, no alternative formula proposed to this point achieves this purpose adequately. It is to be hoped that theologians will soon find a Trinitarian formula which retains the crucial doctrinal affirmations but which is not couched in language that is male-oriented. Until then, we need to be clear about what the ancient terminology does say of central importance to the faith. Three distinctive points are crucial.

i. Father-Son language affirms that God is self-generative, and as such is the source of all life. Early Trinitarian theologians, such as Athanasius, took pains to point out that the Second Person of the Trinity is not *created* by the First Person but, rather, *begotten.* God does not *make* Christ, as a potter makes a bowl; Christ is eternally begotten of God, and all life proceeds from this self-generative nature of the Almighty.

It is difficult to see how this characteristic of God can be expressed metaphorically apart from a parental image. The current substitution of *Creator* for *Father* points in exactly the opposite direction. It does seem to imply that Christ was created in the same way as the world. This is likely to result in a weakened Christology, and all that follows from it. Moreover, in our technological age it is increasingly important to understand that while science may *replicate* life, strictly speaking, scientists cannot *create* life. Even God does not create life but, instead, shares it. The life God generates fills created forms God has made to house it; but life itself is uncreated, and pertains to God alone who is the Uncreated One.

ii. Father-Son language affirms that God is self-consistent. The intimate biological and psychological relationship of parent and child expresses in a unique way the unity of purpose that exists in all that God does. The contemporary substitution of "Creator and Redeemer" fails to express this. A multitude of religions have had a Creator deity and a Redeemer deity who were at odds with each other. The Creator made a mess of things, and the Redeemer had to make the best of a bad situation. Christians emphatically reject such theology as being heretical. The self-consistency of God is particularly crucial with respect to the doctrine of the atonement; without it, the Redeemer is seen as being antagonistic toward the Creator rather than as being a gift and expression of the Creator's love toward the fallen creatures.

iii. Father-Son language affirms that God is personal, not merely functional. Machines can create and sustain things; they function, but they are not persons. This also is a critical point in a technological age. God is personal, and has a rich and mysterious inner being we can only describe as being one of community.

Sometimes it is intimated that creation is the result of God's loneliness: God made us to fill a divine inner need. While this suggestion may be flattering to human beings, it is devastating to a sound doctrine of God. God is not lonely, for God is by nature community. The motive behind creation is absolute love, not neurotic need. This divine fullness which extends into creation is best revealed in the cross. Selfishness seeks to avoid pain; only unselfishness will endure it to the point of utter sacrifice. No more powerful metaphor is likely to be found for unselfish, atoning love than the personal image of a parent who graciously renders up an only child for the sake of others.

The internal, personal richness of God is further emphasized in the interpenetration of God's functions. It is not sufficient to say that the Father creates, the Son redeems, and the Spirit sustains. True Trinitarianism insists that the Father creates, the Son creates, the Spirit creates; the Father redeems, the Son redeems, and so on. Nor does God have only three functions; the richness of the deity implies a multiplicity of functions, as the many appellations for God in Scripture make clear. This point the currently popular formula, "Creator, Redeemer, Sustainer" misses utterly; thereby it easily slips into what is known technically as "the economic heresy."

Despite the archaic nature of the philosophical categories that underlie it, in light of these three considerations concerning God as self-generative, self-consistent, and personal, the Trinitarian formula is an amazing kind of theological shorthand. Particularly as we are incorporated into the Christian faith at baptism, it says far more to us than any other dozen words we have thought of in two thousand years. That the formula should be locked into male imagery is exceedingly regrettable. One could talk about Mother-Daughter-Holy Spirit were it not for the obvious historical fact that Jesus was a male; suggestions that we speak of Mother-Son-Spirit or Father/Mother-Son-Spirit create more problems, theological as well as practical, than they solve.

Theologians are obligated to wrestle with this perplexing matter. We cannot settle for a statement which says less about God than does the historic Trinitarian formula. For the true identity of human beings, male and female, can be known only in light of who God is. Any language that diminishes God by appearing to make the deity less than self-generative, self-consistent, and personal to the extent of being mysteriously complete in being will, at the same time, diminish the identity of both men and woman, no matter how sexually inclusive such language may appear to be.

Because baptism is the sign of our incorporation into God and thus is a crucial clue to the identity that God gives us as those who share the divine image, at the moment of initiation it is imperative that we say as much about God as it is humanly possible to say.

# INDEX OF BIBLICAL PASSAGES

# INDEX OF BIBLICAL PASSAGES

# GENERAL INDEX